Words That Make You Go, "Hmm..."

Walker, Lee M.

Words That Make You Go, "Hmm…"

Copyright © 2013 by Walker House Publishing, Inc.

ISBN 978-0615-85343-7

For

My greatest accomplishment

Nikki

so very proud of you

~and~

Mom and Dad

Dear Reader,

Words That Make You Go, "Hmm..." has been created as a quick reference for wordsmiths of all kinds. When I was a young girl, I was fascinated by words and excelled in English. My love of words and the English language is largely what attracted me to becoming a court reporter. As such for 19 years and part of the legal field for 24, words have played an integral role in my life.

Today, words change as quickly as technology, and it is crucial, as a court reporter, to keep up. This book was developed to assist with words that may hesitate you in your writing or possibly teach you a word that makes *you* go, "Hmm..."

Although you may find entries in this book which seem rather elementary, they were included in an effort to give contrast to a more obscure meaning or usage of another. There are different stages of learning and students of all levels will find this book useful.

We welcome your input. Please join us for interactive discussion on Facebook at my group titled *One Word, Two Words, Apostrophe, Hyphen, OH MY!* You may also reach us by e-mail at editor@walkerhousepublishing.com. We believe that this book and future versions with updated entries will become a staple in your workplace.

Lee M. Walker
Registered Professional Reporter

Bibliography:

Merriam-Webster's Collegiate Dictionary
    Eleventh Edition, 2011

American Heritage Desk Dictionary
    Fifth Edition, 2013

FAA.gov

iafc.org

taser.com

~~~~~~

* Also note that the main entries in this book were derived from Merriam-Webster's Collegiate Dictionary, Eleventh Edition, 2011. An alternate spelling is indicated in parentheses and were derived from American Heritage Desk Dictionary, Fifth Edition, 2013. This book is intended to make the user aware of words that may often confuse or may be looked up repeatedly. This is not intended to be a dictionary, rather a lightweight reference for ease of use. Ample room has been provided for you to make notes for yourself.

—A—

aback
abash
abate
abatement
ABCs
abdicate
abeam
aberrant
abet
abeyance
abhor
abhorrence
abhorrent
abidance
ab initio
abject
abjure
ablate
ablation
ablaze
able-bodied (adj)
able seaman
abloom
abluted
aboard
A-bomb
about-face (n, v)
about-turn
above all
aboveboard (adj, adv)
aboveground (adj)
abovementioned
abracadabra
abreast
absentee ballot
absentminded
absolute zero
abubble

abutment
abutting
abuzz
abysmal
Abyssinian
A/C
a cappella (also a capella)
accident-prone (adj)
accoutrement
AC/DC
ACE bandage
ACE inhibitor
Achilles' heel
Achilles tendon
achiness
achy
acidhead
acid rain
acid snow
acid-washed
acknowledgment
acne rosacea
acquit
acquittal
acquittance
acreage
across-the-board (adj)
active-matrix
activewear
actual cash value
acumen
acupressure
acupuncture
Adam's apple
add-in (n, adj)
Addison's disease
addlepated
add-on (n, adj)
adenocarcinoma
adenovirus

ad hoc
ad hominem
ad infinitum
adipose tissue
Adirondack chair
adjuvant therapy
ad lib (adv)
ad-lib (v, adj)
ad loc
ad nauseum
adnexa
Adrenalin ™ (chemical adrenaline)
adrenaline (naturally occurring)
adult-onset diabetes
ad valorem
advanced degree
advance directive
adware
aerobatics
aesthetic
aesthetician
afar
afebrile
affective disorder
affenpinscher
affidavit
affirmative action
affray
affright
affront
Afghan hound
aficionada (afficionada)
aficionado (afficionado)
afield
afire
aflame
AFL-CIO
afloat
aflutter
afoot

aforementioned
aforethought
afoul of
A-frame
African-American
African gray (bird)
African violet
Afro-American
Afro-Asiatic
Afrocentric
after all
afterbirth
afterburner
aftercare
aftereffect
afterglow
after-hours (adj)
afterlife
aftermarket
aftermath
aftermost
afternoon
after-party
aftershave
aftershock
aftertaste
after-tax (adj)
afterthought
afterward
afterword
age-group (n)
ageless
agelong
age-mate
age-old
aglare
aglitter
aglow
a-go-go
agoraphobia

agranulocyte
agribusiness
agribusinessman
agroecology
agroforestry
agro-industrial
ahold
ahoy
AIDS
AIDS-related complex
AIDS virus
ailment
aioli
air bag (also airbag)
air ball (sports)
air base
airboat
airborne
air brake
air-breathing (adj)
airbrush
airbus
air chief marshal
air conditioner (the physical unit)
air-condition (v)
air-conditioning (n)
aircraft
aircraft carrier
aircrew
air-cushion vehicle
air dam
airdate
airdrome
airdrop (n)
air-drop (v)
air-dry (adj, v)
Airedale terrier
airfare
airfield
airflow

air force
airfreight
airglow
air guitar
air gun
airhead
airhole
air-kiss
air lane
airlift
airline
airliner
airmail
airman
airman first class
air marshal
air mattress
airmobile
airpark
air piracy
airplane
airplay
air pocket
air police
airport
airpower
air rage
air raid
air rifle
air sac
air show
airsick
airspace
airspeed
airstream
airstrip
air taxi
airtight
airtime
air-to-air

air vice-marshal
airwave
airway
airworthy
aisleway
aka (also known as)
AKC (American Kennel Club)
AK-47
Akita
a la carte
a la king
a la mode
Alaskan malamute (dog)
albacore
albatross
albeit
albumen (white of an egg)
albumin (re: multiple proteins)
albuterol
alcopop
al dente
alehouse
alexander (cocktail)
Alfa (communications code for letter A)
alfresco
algorithm
alienation
A-line
A-list
aliteracy
alkali metal
all-American (n)
all-around (adj)
allay
all clear (n)
alleluia
all-embracing
Allen wrench
alley cat
alley-oop

alleyway
all-encompassing
all get-out
all-inclusive
all-knowing
all-important
all-inclusive
all-night (adj)
all-nighter
allograft
allonge (n, contracts)
allongé (adj, ballet)
allopathic
allopurinol
all-or-none
all-or-nothing
allotment
all-out
all-powerful
all-purpose
all-seeing
allspice
all-star (n, adj)
all-terrain vehicle
all-time
all told
alma mater
almighty
Almighty (when referring to God)
almond-eyed
almsman (charity recipient)
aloe vera
aloft
alongshore
alongside
aloof
alpha-adrenergic
alpha and omega
alpha-fetoprotein
alpha globulin

alpha-helix
alphanumeric
alpha particle
alpha-receptor
altar boy
altar call
altarpiece
alter ego
altruism
Alzheimer's disease
amass
Amber Alert
ambidextrous
ambulance chaser
amebic dysentery (also amoebic)
amenorrhea
Amerasian
American dream
American foxhound
American Indian
American pit bull terrier
American saddlebred
American shorthair (cat)
American Sign Language
American Staffordshire terrier
American water spaniel
Ames test
amici curiae
amicus curiae
amino acid
aminoaciduria
aminobenzoic acid
aminosalicylic acid
aminotransferase
amiss
amniotic fluid
amniotic sac
amok (also amuck)
ampere-hour
ampere-turn

amperometric
ampersand
amphitheater
amuse-bouche
AMVETS
anabolic steroid
anaerobic
anal-retentive
anaphylactic shock
Anatolian shepherd
anchorman
anchorpeople
anchorperson
anchorwoman
Andalusian (horse)
and/or
anew
angelfish
angel food cake
angel-hair pasta
anglerfish
angleworm
Anglo-American
Anglo-Catholic
Anglocentric
Anglo-French
Anglo-Saxon
angora (sweater)
Angora cat
Angora goat
Angora rabbit
Anjou pear
anklebone
anorexia nervosa
anoxic
ANSI (American National Standards Institute)
anteater
antechamber
antemortem
antenatal

ante-post
anterior cruciate ligament (ACL)
anteroom
anti-American
anti-art
anti-federalist
anti-idiotype
anti-inflammatory
anti-intellectual
anti-roll bar
anti-Semitism
anti-utopia
any more (referring to quantity)
anymore (referring to time)
A-OK
Apgar score
apiece
aplenty
Appaloosa (horse)
apple-pie (adj)
applet (computer app)
Aqua-Lung ™
aquamarine
aquascape
aqueduct
aquifer
aquiver
arachnophobia
Arborio rice
archbishop
archdiocese
archenemy
archetype
archrival
arctic char
Arctic Circle
area code
areaway
ARM (adjustable rate mortgage)
arm and a leg (expensive)

armband
arm candy
arm-chair (n)
armchair (adj)
armed forces
armed services
armful
armpit
armrest
arm's length (n)
arms-length (adj)
arm-twisting (n)
aromatherapy
around-the-clock (adj)
arrowhead
arrowroot
art deco
art nouveau
artsy-craftsy
artwork
aseptic
asexual
ashore
ashtray
Asian-American
Asperger's syndrome
asphyxia
asphyxiate
assay (n, v, analyze)
assembly-line (adj)
assembly line (n)
assistant professor
assisted living
Associate of Science (cap the specialty)
associate professor
associate's degree
associate's in science (uncap the specialty)
associate's of science (uncap the specialty)
astarboard (starboardside)
astrobiology

at-home (adj)
at-large
attack dog
attackman
attention deficit disorder
attention-deficit/hyperactivity disorder
attorney-at-law
attorney-client privilege
attorney-client relationship
audiobook
audiovisual
auld lang syne
au pair (nanny)
Australian cattle dog
Australian shepherd
Australian terrier
autobahn
autobiography
autocorrect (not in dictionaries, but often used)
autoimmune
automaker
automatic teller machine (ATM)
autonomic nervous system
autoworker
A/V (audio/video)
avant-garde
avascular necrosis
Ave Maria
A-V node
a while (when used with "for")
awhile
AWOL (absent without leave)
aw-shucks

—B—

baba ghanoush
Babinski reflex
baby boom
babysat
babysit

babysitter
babysitting
Bachelor of Science (cap the specialty)
bachelor's degree
bachelor's in science (uncap the specialty)
bachelor's of science (uncap the specialty)
backache
back-and-forth (n)
back and forth (adv)
backbite
backboard
backbone
back brace
backbreaking
back burner (n)
back-burner (v)
backcountry
backcourt
backdate
back dive
backdoor (adj)
back door (n)
backdrop
backfill
backfire (n, v)
backflip
backflow
backgammon
background
backhand
backhanded
backhoe
backhouse
backlash
backlight
backlist
backlog
back-office (adj)
back-order (v)
back order (n)

backpack
backpedal
backroom (adj)
back room (n)
back-scratching (n)
backseat
backseat driver
backside (n)
backslap
backslash
backspace
backsplash
backstab
backstabber
backstabbing
backstage
backstairs
backstitch
backstop
backstreet
backstretch
backstroke
backswimmer
backswing
back talk
backtrack
back up (v)
backup (n)
backward
backwash
backwoods
backyard
badminton
bad-mouth (v)
bad-mouthing
bag lady
bagman
bagpipe
Bahia grass
bailiwick

bailout (n)
bail out (v)
bailsman
bain-marie
bait and switch (n)
baitfish
baker's dozen
bakeware
bald-faced (also bold-faced)
baldhead (n)
bald-headed (adj)
ball-and-socket joint
ball bearing
ballbuster
ballcarrier
ball game
ball joint
ballot box
ballpark
ball-peen hammer
ballplayer
ballroom
ballroom dancing
balustrade
banana republic
Banana Republic ™
bananas Foster
Band-Aid ™
B and B (bed-and-breakfast)
band shell
bandstand
b and w (black and white)
bandwidth
bankbook
bank card
banknote
bankroll
bantamweight
barback
barbell

barbershop
barbwire (barbed wire)
bar code (barcode)
bareback
bare bones (n)
barebones (adj)
barefoot
barefooted
barehand (v, baseball)
bare-handed
bare-knuckle
bare-knuckled
barfly
bargain-basement (adj)
bargain basement (n)
barhop
barmaid
bar mitzvah
bar mitzvahed
bar mitzvahing
barnyard (n, adj)
barstool
baseball
baseboard
BASE jumping
baseline
base pay
baseplate
basketball
basketballer
basket case
basketful
basketlike
basketwork
basmati rice
basset hound
bathhouse
bathing suit
bathmat
bathrobe

bathroom
bath salts
bathtub
bathwater
bat mitzvah
bat mitzvahed
bat mitzvahing
battered child syndrome
battered woman syndrome
battery-operated
battle-ax
battlefield
battlefront
battleground
battle line
battleship
Bavarian cream
bay leaf
bay rum
bay scallop
bay window
beach ball
beachboy
beach buggy
beachcomber
beachfront
beachgoer
beach grass
beachside
beach towel
beachwear
beadwork
beagle (dog)
be-all and end-all
beanbag
bean counter
bean curd (tofu)
beanpole
bearded collie (dog)
bear-hug (v)

bear hug (n)
beatnik
bed-and-breakfast
bedbug
bed-hop (v)
bedmate
bedpan
bedpost
bed rest
bedridden
bedrock
bedroom
bedsheet
bedside
bedsore
bedspread
bedspring
bedtime
bed wetter
bed-wetting (n)
beefcake
beefsteak
beefsteak tomato
beef Stroganoff
beef Wellington
beehive
beekeeper
beeline
beer belly
beer pong
bee's knees
bee-sting
bee-stung
beeswax
befall
befitting
before-and-after (n)
beforehand
before long
begrudge

behind-the-scenes (adj)
bejeweled
Belgian Malinois (dog)
Belgian sheepdog
Belgian Tervuren
bell-bottoms
bellboy
bell captain
bell curve
bellflower
bellhop
bells and whistles
bell-shaped
Bell's palsy
bell tower
bellyache
belly button
belly dance
belly flop
bellyful
belly laugh
belly-up (adj)
belly up (v)
belowground
belt-tightening (n)
beltway
benchmark
bench press
bench seat
benchwarmer
bench warrant
Bengal tiger
BENGAY ™
Bermuda grass
Bermuda shorts
Bernese mountain dog
berserk
best-case (adj)
best seller (n)
best-selling (adj)

beta-blocker
beta-carotene
bias-belted tire
bias-ply tire
Bibb lettuce
Bible Belt (ref. geography)
Bible-thumper
Bible-thumping
bicep
biceps
biceps brachii
biceps femoris
bichon frise (dog)
bicipital
bicoastal
bicolored
bicultural
bicuspid
bicuspid valve
bidirectional
biennial
biennium
bifocal
bifold
bifurcate
big bang theory
Big Ben
big-box (adj)
Big C (cancer)
Big Dipper
bigeye tuna
bigfoot
bighearted
Big House (prison)
big shot
big-ticket (adj)
big-time (adj)
bigwig
bi-level (n, adj)
bilge keel (marine)

bilge water (marine)
bilirubin
billabong
billboard
billfish
billfold
billhook
bill of health
bill of lading
bill of particulars
Bill of Rights (government, Constitution preamble)
bill of rights (medical, a patient's bill of rights)
bill of sale
billy club
billy goat
bimonthly
Binet-Simon scale
biodefense
biodegradable
biodiesel
biodynamics
bioengineer
biofeedback
bioflavonoid
biofuel
biohazard
bioinformatics
biological clock
bioluminescence
biomechanics
biomedical
biometrics
biomimetics
BIOS (Basic Input/Output System)
biotechnology
biotelemetry
bioterrorism
biowarfare
biowaste
bioweapon

bipartisan
biplane
bipolar
bipolar disorder
biracial
birdbath
birdbrain
birdbrained
birdcage
birdcall
bird-dog (v)
bird dog (n)
bird-dogging
bird flu
birdhouse
birdie (golf)
bird of paradise (bird)
bird-of-paradise (plant)
bird of prey
birdseed
bird's-eye view
bird's-nest fern
bird's nest soup
birdsong
bird-watch
bird-watcher
birth date
birthmark
birth mother
birthplace
birthrate
birthright
birthstone
bisect
bisexual
bite plate
bite-size (adj)
bite-sized (adj)
bitewing
bitter end (n)

bittersweet
bivalve
biweekly
biyearly
bizarro
bizonal
blabbermouth
black-and-blue (adj)
black-and-white (adj)
black and white (n)
Black Angus
blackball
blackberry (fruit)
blackberries (fruit)
BlackBerry ™
BlackBerrys ™
blackbird
blackboard
black box
black cherry
black eye (n)
black-eyed pea
black hole
black ice
blackjack
black light
blacklist
blackmail
black-market (v)
black market (n)
black-on-black
blackout (n)
black out (v)
black raspberry
blacksmith
black-tie (adj)
black tie (n)
blacktop
bleary-eyed (adj)
blind carbon copy

blindfold
bling-bling
B-list
blockbuster
blockhead
blockhouse
block party
blogosphere
blond
blood-and-guts (adj)
bloodbath
blood-borne (adj)
bloodcurdling
bloodhound
bloodline
bloodmobile
blood poisoning
blood pressure
bloodred
bloodshed
bloodshot
bloodstain
bloodstained
bloodstream
bloodsucker
bloodthirsty
blood-typing (n)
bloodworm
Bloody Mary (cocktail)
Bloody Marys (plural)
bloody murder
blowback
blowby
blow-by-blow (adj)
blow-dried
blow-dry
blow-dryer
blowfish
blowhole
blowout (n)

blow out (v)
blowtorch
blowup (n)
blow up (v)
bluebird
bluebonnet (n)
blue-collar (adj)
Blue Cross and Blue Shield
blue-eyed (adj)
bluefin tuna
blue jay
blue-ribbon (adj)
blue ribbon (n)
Bluetooth ™
Blu-ray ™
Blu-ray Disc ™
boardinghouse
boarding school
boardman
boardroom
boardsailing
boardwalk
boatbuilder
boathouse
boatload
boatman
boatneck
boatshoe
boatswain
boatyard
bobblehead doll
bobsledding
body bag
bodyboard
bodybuilding
bodyguard
body language
body shop
bodysuit
bodysurf

bodywash
bodywork
bogeyman
boilerplate
boiler room
bok choy
boldface (bold print)
bold-faced (bold manner)
Bollywood
bombshell
bona fide
bondholder
bondsman
bone-chilling
bone-dry (adj)
bonefish
Bonefish Grill ™
bonehead
bone marrow
bonfire
boo-boo
booby trap
boogie-woogie
bookbinding
bookcase
book club
bookend
bookkeeper
bookkeeping
bookmaker
bookmark
bookseller
bookshelf
bookstore
bookworm
boomtown
boondocks
boot camp
bootleg
bootstrap

borderline
border terrier
born-again (adj)
Boston cream pie
Boston lettuce
Boston terrier
bottle blond
bottlebrush
bottle-feed
bottleneck
bottlenose dolphin
bottom-feeder
bottom-line (adj)
bottom line (n)
bottommost
bougainvillea
bouillabaisse
bowleg
bowlegged
bowline
bow tie
boxcar
box cutter
boxer (dog & fighter)
box lunch
box office
box seat
box spring
box turtle
bradycardia
brain-dead (adj)
brainpower
brain stem
brainstorm
brainwash
brain wave
brand-name (adj)
brand name (n)
brand-new (adj)
brand new (n)

Bravo (communications code for letter B)
bread-and-butter (adj)
bread and butter (n)
breadbasket
breadwinner
break down (v)
breakdown (n)
breakeven (n)
break-even (adj)
break-in (n)
break in (v)
breakneck
breakout (n)
break out (v)
break room
breakthrough (n)
break through (v)
breakup (n)
break up (v)
breastbone
breastplate
breaststroke
Breathalyzer ™
breathtaking
breezeway
brick-and-mortar (adj)
brick house
bricklayer
brick wall
brickwork
brickyard
bridegroom
bridesmaid
bridgework
bright-line (adj)
Bright's disease
brimstone
broadband
broad-brush (adj)
broadcast

broad-minded (adj)
broadside
broad-spectrum (adj)
broccoli rabe
brokenhearted
bronchodilator
bronchoscope
bronchospasm
broomstick
brotherhood
brother-in-law
browbeat
brownnose
brownstone
brushfire (adj)
brush fire (n)
brush-off (n)
brussels sprout
bubblegum (adj)
bubble gum (n)
bubblehead
bubbleheaded
Bubble Wrap ™
bucket seat
buckeye
Buckeye (Ohio native)
bucksaw
buckshot
buckskin
buckskinned
bucktooth
buckwheat
Buddha
Buddhism
buddy-buddy
bug-eyed
buildup (n)
build up (v)
built-in (n, adj)
built-up (adj)

bulgur wheat
bulkhead
bulldog
bulldoze
bulldozer
bulletproof
bullfight
bullfighting
bullfrog
bullhorn
bullmastiff
bull pen
bull's-eye
bull terrier
bullwhip
bully pulpit
bumblebee
bumper-to-bumper (adj)
bumpkin
bum-rush
bunco
Bundt ™
bungee jump
bunk bed
bupkus
burglarproof
burned-out (adj)
burnout (n)
burn out (v)
burnt-out (adj)
busboy
bushman
bushmaster
bushwhack
businesslike
businessman
businesspeople
businessperson
businesswoman
busload

busybody
busywork
butcher block
but for
butterball
buttercream
buttercup
butterfat
butterfly
butter lettuce
buttermilk
butternut
butterscotch
button-down (adj)
buttoned-up (adj)
buttonhole
buyback
buyout (n)
buy out (v)
buzzkill
buzzword
by-and-by (n)
by and by (adv)
bye-bye
bygone
bylaw
byline
bypass
by-product
bystander
byway

—C—

cabdriver
cabinetmaker (n)
cabinetwork
cabin fever
cable-knit
cabstand
cakewalk

calla lily
callback
call-in (adj)
call in (v)
call sheet
call sign
call-waiting
CAM (common area maintenance)
camelback
cameraman
cameraperson
camerawoman
campfire
campground
campsite
camshaft
cam wheel
candleholder
candlelight
candlelit
candlesnuffer
candlestick
candlewick
candlewood
canon law
cantilever
can't-miss (adj)
canvas (n, a cover, also canvass)
canvass (v, to search an area, also canvas)
captain's chair
cardboard
card-carrying (adj)
cardholder
carefree
caregiver
careless
care package
caretaker
carfare
cargo pants

carjacking
carload
carmaker
carnauba wax
carpe diem
carpool (v)
car pool (n)
carport
carry-on (adj, n)
carry on (v)
carryout (n)
carry out (v)
carryover (adj)
carry over (v)
car seat
carsick
carte blanche
cartwheel
case in point
case law
caseload
case study
casework
cash-and-carry (n, adj)
cash cow
cash-strapped
castaway
catacorner
cata-cornered
catchall (n)
catch-as-catch-can (n, wrestling) (adj, hit-or-miss)
catchphrase
catch-22
catch-22s
catch-up (n, adj)
catch up (v)
catercorner
cater-cornered
catfish
catnap

catnip
CAT scan
cat scratch disease
catsuit
cattle prod
catty-corner
catty-cornered
catwalk
Cavalier King Charles spaniel
caveat emptor
CD-ROM
cease and desist
cease-fire (n)
celiac disease
cell phone (cellphone)
censorship
center field
centerfold
centerline
center of gravity
centerpiece
center stage
Central time
cerebrospinal
cesspool
chain gang
chain-link fence
chain reaction
chain saw (n)
chainsaw (v)
chain-smoke
chain-smoker
chairman
chairperson
chairwoman
chaise lounge
chalkboard
chalk up
challah bread
changeover (n)

channel surfing
Chanukah (also Hanukkah)
Chapter 7 (bankruptcy)
Chapter 11 (bankruptcy)
Chapter 13 (bankruptcy)
charge-off (n)
charge off (v)
charley horse
Charlie (communications code for letter C)
chateaubriand
chatterbox
cheapskate
cheat sheet
checkbook
checkerboard
check-in (n)
check in (v)
checklist
checkmark
checkmate
cherry-pick (v)
cherry picker (n)
Chesapeake Bay retriever
chessboard
chest-thumping
chicken-fried steak
chickpea
Chihuahua
childbearing
childlike
childproof
child's play
Chili's ™
Chinese drywall
Chinese shar-pei
chip shot
chitchat
check out (v)
checkout (n)
chock-full or chockful

choirmaster
chophouse
chop shop
chopstick
chotchke (tchotchke)
chowhound
Christmastime
chutzpah
Cinco de Mayo
circuit board
circuit breaker
cityscape
citywide
civic-minded
clambake
clamshell
class action (n)
class-action (adj)
classmate
classroom
clayware
clean-cut
cleanup (adj)
clean up (v)
clear-cut (n, adj)
clearheaded
clearinghouse
cleft lip
cleft palate
cliff-hang (v)
cliff-hanger (n)
clipboard
clip-clop
clocklike
clockwise
clockwork
clodhopper
close-cropped
closed-captioned
closed-captioning

close-in (adj)
close-knit
closemouthed
closeout (n)
close out (v)
close-up (n, adv, adj)
clot-buster (n)
cloud computing
clubfoot
clubfooted
clubhouse
clumber spaniel
C-note ($100 bill)
coastline
coast-to-coast (adj)
coatrack
coatroom
coattail
cobblestone
Cobb salad
Coca-Cola ™
cockamamy
cockapoo (dog)
cockatiel (bird)
cockatoo (bird)
cocker spaniel
cockeye
cockeyed
cockroach
codebook
code name
code word
codfish
cod-liver oil
coffee break
coffee cake
coffee hour
coffeehouse
coffee klatch (coffee-klatsch)
coffeemaker

coffeepot
coffee shop
coffee-table (adj)
coffee table (n)
cold-blooded (adj)
cold call
cold cash
cold cuts
coldhearted
cold-press (v)
Coldwell Banker
color-blind (adj)
color blindness
colorectal
comeback (n)
come-on (n)
come on (v)
comeuppance
comity of nations
committeeman
committeewoman
common-law (adj)
common law (n)
commonplace
common sense (n)
commonsense (adj)
commonwealth
compos mentis
computernik
confectioners' sugar
congressman
congresspeople
congressperson
congresswoman
contact lens
contact lenses
contretemps
convenience store
cookbook
cookie-cutter (adj)

cookie cutter (n)
cookie sheet
cook-off (n)
cook off (v)
cookout
cooktop
cookware
cooldown (n)
coolheaded (adj)
coonhound (dog)
coop (poultry pen)
co-op
co-pay
co-payment
copilot
cop-out (n)
cop out (v)
copperhead
copter (helicopter)
copycat
copyright
copywriter
corgi (dog)
corkboard
corkscrew
corncob
corn dog
cornerback
corner kick
cornerman
cornerwise
corn-fed
cornfield
cornflakes
Cornhusker (Nebraska native)
Cornish hen
cornmeal
cornrow
corn silk
cornstarch

corn syrup
corporate-wide
corpsman
corpus delicti
corticosteroid
cost-benefit (adj)
cost-effective (adj)
cost-efficient (adj)
cotton candy
cottonmouth
cotton-picking (adj)
cottonseed
cottontail
counselor-at-law
counterbalance
counterchange
counter check (banking)
countercheck (v)
counterclaim
counterclockwise
counterfeit
counterintelligence
counterman
countermeasure
counteroffer
counterpart
counterproductive
countertop
counterweight
country-club (adj)
country club (n)
countryside
countrywide
court-martial (n, v)
courthouse
courtroom
courtship
courtside
courtyard
coverall (n)

cover girl
cover-up (n)
cowhide
cowlick
cowl-neck
coworker
cowpoke
coxswain
crabgrass
crabmeat
crack-down (n)
crack down (v)
cracker-barrel (adj)
Cracker Barrel ™
crackerjack (n)
crackhead
crack house
crackpot
cradle cap
craftsman
craftsmanlike
craftspeople
craftsperson
craftswoman
craigslist ™
crankcase
crapshoot
crash cart
crash-land (v)
crashworthy
crawfish
crawl space
crayfish
C-reactive protein
crew chief
crew cut
crewman
crewmate
crisscross (adj, adv, n)
Crock-Pot ™

Crohn's disease
crop-eared (adj)
cropland
crossability
crossable
cross action
crossbanding
crossbar
crossbeam
crossbearer
crossbill
crossbones
crossbow
crossbowman
crossbred
crossbreed
cross-check (n, v)
cross-claim
cross-country (n, adj)
crosscourt
cross-cultural
crosscurrent
crosscut (n, v, adj)
crosscutting
cross-dress
cross-dresser
cross-dressing
cross-examine
cross-examiner
cross-examination
cross-eye
cross-eyed
cross-eyes
cross-fertilization
cross-fertilize
cross fire
CrossFit ™
crosshair
crosshatch
crosshead

cross-index
crossing-over
cross-legged
crosslet
crosslinguistic
cross-link
cross multiply
cross-national
crossopterygian
cross over (v)
crossover (n, adj)
cross-ownership
crosspatch
crosspiece
cross-plaintiff
cross-pollinate
cross-purpose
cross-question
cross-reaction
cross-reference (n, v)
crossroad
crossroad-utility vehicle (CUV)
crossruff
cross section (n)
cross-section (v)
cross-staff
cross-stitch
cross street
cross talk
cross-tolerance
crosstown
cross-trade
cross-train
cross-trainer
crosstrees
crosswalk
crossway
crosswind
crosswise
cross word (meaning harsh word)

crossword (a puzzle)
crowd-pleaser (n)
crowdsourcing
crow's-foot (wrinkles)
cruelty-free
cruiserweight
crumple zone
crybaby
C-section
C-spine (cervical spine)
cubbyhole
cuff link
cul-de-sac
cum laude
cupboard
cuplike
curative instruction
curbside
cure-all (n)
curly-coated retriever
curriculum vitae
curtain-raiser
Cushing's disease
custom-built (adj)
custom-made (adj)
custom-tailor (v)
cut-and-dried (adj)
cut-and-dry (adj)
cut-and-paste (adj)
cutback (n)
cut back (v)
cutoff (n)
cut off (v)
cutout (n)
cut out (v, adj)
cut-rate (adj)
cutthroat (n, adj)
cuttlebone
CUV (crossroad-utility vehicle)
CVS/pharmarcy ™

cyberbullying
cybercafe
cyberporn
cybersecurity
cybersex
cyberspace
cyberspeak
cybersurfer
cyberterrorism
cystic fibrosis

—D—

dachshund (dog)
daddy longlegs
Dalai Lama
dalmatian
Dandie Dinmont terrier
Danish (pastry)
daredevil
Darjeeling tea
darkroom
dashboard
data bank
database
date-rape (v)
date rape (n)
date rape drug
daybed
daybreak
day care
daydream
dayflower
Day-Glo ™
dayglow
day job
day laborer
daylight
daylight saving time
daylong
daymare

dayroom
day school
daytime
day-to-day (adj)
day trader
day-tripper
deadbeat
dead-end (adj, v)
dead end (n)
deadhead
deadline
deadlock
dead man's float
dead-on (adj)
deadweight
dean's list
Dear John letter
deathbed
death trap
death wish
deckhand
deckhouse
decubitus ulcer
de-emphasize
de-energize
deep-dish (adj)
Deepfreeze ™
deep-freeze (v)
deep freeze (n)
deep-fry (v)
deep fryer
deep-rooted (adj)
deep-sea (adj)
deep-seated
deep-six (v)
deep six (n)
deepwater (adj)
deerhound (dog)
DEF-CON
delivery boy

deliveryman
Delta (communications code for letter D)
demi-glace
de minimis
demi-sec
demitasse
depth perception
desktop
de-stress
deutsche mark
devil's advocate
diabetes insipidus
diabetes mellitus
diamondhead
diatribe
Dictaphone ™
diddly-squat
die-hard (adj)
Dijon mustard
dime novel
dime-store (adj)
dime store (n)
dim sum
dimwit
dim-witted
ding-a-ling (n)
dingbat
ding-dong (n, v, adj)
diphtheria
diphthong
direct examination
dirtbag
dirt-poor
disc jockey
dishcloth
dishpan
dishpan hands
dishrag
dishwasher
dishwater

disklike
dissociative identity disorder
dive-bomb (v)
diving board
diving suit
Doberman pinscher
dockhand
dockmaster
dockside
dockworker
dockyard
doctor-patient (as in relationship)
dodgeball
doe-eyed
dog and pony show
dogcatcher
dog-ear (n, v)
dog-eat-dog
dogfight
doggie bag
doghouse
do-good (adj)
do-gooder
dogsled
dog tag
dogtooth
d'oh
do-it-yourself
dojo
dollars-and-cents (adj)
dollhouse
domain name
domino effect
done deal
done for
doodlebug
doodly-squat
doorway
Doppler effect
Doppler radar

do-rag
do-si-do
do-si-dos
double agent
double-barrel (n)
double-barreled (adj)
double-blind (adj)
double-breasted (adj)
double-cross (v)
double cross (n)
double-decker
double-digit (adj)
double-dipper (n)
double-edged
double-ended
doubleheader
double helix
double jeopardy
double-jointed
double negative
double-park
double-space (v)
double standard
double-talk
double-team
double-time
double-wide (n)
dovetail
down-and-out (adj)
downdraft
downgrade
downhill
down-home
download
down-market
downplay
downpour
downright
downriver
downscale

downshift
downside
downsize
downslope
downstream
downstroke
downswing
Down syndrome
down-to-earth (adj)
down-to-the-wire (adj)
downtown
downtrend
downtrodden
downturn
Down Under (ref. to Australia)
downward
downwind
draftsman
draftsperson
drag-and-drop (adj)
dragline
dragonfly
drag race
drainpipe
drawback
drawbridge
drawdown
drawing board
drawstring
dreadlock
dreamboat
dreamscape
dreamworld
dress-down day
drill press
drip-dry (v, adj)
drive-by (adj, n)
drive-bys
drive-in (n)
drive-through (n, also, drive-thru)

drivetrain
drive-up (adj)
driveway
driving range
drop box (n)
Dropbox ™
drop cloth
drop-dead (adj)
drop-down (adj)
drop-in (n)
dropkick (n)
drop-kick (v)
drop-off (n)
drop off (v)
dropout (n)
drop out (v)
drop-ship (v)
drop-top (n)
drugmaker
drugstore
drumbeat
drum brake
drumroll
dry-clean (v)
dry cleaner
dry cleaning
dry-dock (v)
dry dock (n)
dry-erase board
dry-rot (v)
dry rot (n)
drywall
dual citizenship
Duchenne muscular dystrophy
ductwork
due diligence
due process
duffel bag
dugout
du jour

dumbbell
dumbfound
dumbstruck
dumbwaiter
Dumpster ™
dump truck
dune buggy
Dungeness crab
Dunkin' Donuts ™
dura mater
durum wheat
dustcover
dust mite
dustpan

—E—

earache
earbud
ear canal
ear clip
eardrum
Earl Grey tea
earlobe
early bird
earmark
earmuff
earphone
earpiece
earplug
earshot
earsplitting
earthenware
earthquake
earth-shattering
earth tone
earthworm
earwax
earwig
east (referring to direction)
East (referring to a region; i.e., East Chicago)

Eastern Hemisphere
easternmost
Eastern time
east-northeast
east-southeast
easygoing
easy peasy
easy street
eau-de-vie
eavesdrop
EBITDA (earnings before interest, taxes,
          depreciation, and amortization)
Ebola virus
e-book
Echo (communications code for E)
eco-conscious
eco-friendly
E. coli
e-commerce
edgewise
editor in chief
eggbeater
egghead
eggnog
eggplant
eggs Benedict
eggshell
egomaniac
ego trip
18-wheeler
800 number
eightpenny nail
either-or
e-mail (email)
embankment
emoticon
empty-handed (adj)
empty nester
empty-nest syndrome
en banc (Lat., adj, in full court)

54

endcap
endgame
endnote
end plate
end-stage (adj)
end table
end user
English setter (dog)
en masse (as a whole)
entranceway
entry-level (adj)
entryway
Epsom salt
Epstein-Barr virus
ERISA (Employee Retirement Income Security Act)
Ethernet
E*TRADE ™
even-keeled (adj)
even-steven
every day (each day)
everyday (adj, i.e., everyday prices)
evildoer
evil-minded
Ewing's sarcoma
ex post facto
extracurricular
extramarital
extravasate
eyeball
eyeball-to-eyeball (adj, adv)
eyebrow
eye candy
eye-catcher
eye chart
eye contact
eyecup
eyedness
eyedropper
eyedrops
eyeful

eyeglass
eyeglasses
eyehole
eyelash
eyelet
eyelid
eye lift
eyeliner
eye-opener
eyepiece
eyepopper
eye shadow
eyeshot
eyesight
eye socket
eyesore
eyestrain
eyetooth
eye view
eyewash
eyewear
eyewitness
e-zine

—F—

Facebook ™
facecloth
facedown (adv)
face-first (adv, adj)
face-lift
face mask
face-off (n)
face off (v)
faceplate
face-to-face (adv, adj)
faceup (adv)
face up (adv)
face value
fact-check (v)
fact finder

fade-in (n)
fade-out (n)
fail-safe (adj, n)
fainthearted
fairground
fair-haired
fair market value
fair-minded
fair-weather (adj)
fairy-tale (adj)
fairy tale (n)
fait accompli
fallback (n)
fall back (v)
fall guy
falling-out (n)
falltime
false start
fancy-free
fancy-pants
fanfare
fantail
fantasyland
far and away
far and wide
faraway (adj)
farbisener
far cry
farewell
far-fetched
far-flung
farmhand
farmhouse
farmland
farmstead
farmwife
farmworker
farmyard
far-out (adj)
far-reaching

farseeing
farside (n)
farsighted
farsightedness
farthermost
fast-food (adj)
fast-forward (n, v)
fast-talker
fast-track (adj, v)
fast track (n)
fathead
Fat Tuesday
faux pas
feather bed (n)
featherweight
feedback
fee-for-service (n)
feel-good (adj)
fender bender
feng shui
Ferris wheel
festivalgoer
fetal alcohol syndrome
fettucine Alfredo
fiberglass
field spaniel
field-test (v)
field trip
fieldwork
fight-or-flight (adj)
figurehead
figure skating
FIFO (first in, first out)
filibuster
fill-in (n)
fill in (v)
filmmaker
fine-tooth comb
fine-tune
fingernail

finger-pointing
fingerprint
fingertip
firearm
fireball
firecracker
fire-eater
fire-engine red
firefighter
firehouse (fire station)
fireman
fireplace
firepower
fireproof (adj, v)
fire-rescue
fire-sale (adj)
fire sale (n)
fireside
fire station (firehouse)
firetrap
firewall
firmware
first aid
first aid kit
firstborn
first-class (adj)
first class (n)
first-degree burn
firsthand
first-rate (adj, adv)
First World
fish-and-chips
fishbowl
fishmonger
fishtail
fistfight (n)
five-and-ten
fivefold
Five Guys ™
fivesome

five-spice powder
five-star (adj)
flabbergast
flagpole
flame-retardant (adj)
flamethrower
flapjack
flare-up (n)
flashback (n)
flash card
flash mob
flatbed
flatfoot
flat-footed
flatline
flaxseed
fleabag
fleabite
flip-flop (n, v)
flip-flopped
flipside
floodgate
floodlight
floodwater
floorboard
floor-length
flowchart
flowerpot
flu-like
flyby (n)
fly-by-night (n, adj)
flybys
fly-fishing
flypaper
flyswatter
folklore
folksinger
folk song
folktale
follow-up (n, adj)

follow up (v)
foolproof
fool's gold
foot-and-mouth disease
footbath
footboard
foothill
footlocker
footloose
footnote
footprint
footrest
footstool
footwear
footwork
Ford F-150
Ford F-250
Ford F-350
forearm
forecast
foreclose
foreclosure
forego
foregoing
foreground
foreman
foremost
forethought
forevermore
forewarn
forget-me-not (n)
forklift
for-profit (adj)
forthright
forthwith
fortune-teller
fortune-telling
forward-looking
foulmouthed
foul play

fountainhead
fountain pen
401(k)
four-door
fourfold
fourplex
foursome
four-wheel drive
four-wheeler
foxhole
foxhound
foxhunting
foxtail
fox terrier
Foxtrot (communications code for F)
fox-trot (n, v)
framework
frankincense
freebase
free-climb
free diver
free-floating
free-flowing
free-for-all
free-form
freehand
freelance
freeload
Freemason
freemasonry
free-range
freestyle
freeway
freewheeling
freeze-dried
freeze-dry
freeze-frame
French bulldog
French curve
French fry (n, v)

French kiss
French press
French toast
Frenchwoman
Freon ™
freshwater
Freudian slip
front end (n)
front-end (adj)
frontline
front-page (adj, v)
front-runner
front seat
front yard
frostbite
fullback
full-blown (adj)
full-court press
full-fledged
full-length
full nelson
full-scale (adj)
full-service (adj)
full-size (adj)
full-term (adj)
full-time (adj)
full time (n)
full-timer
Fu Manchu
fund-raiser
fund-raising

—G—

gallbladder
gallstone
gamebird
game face
gamesmanship
gangbuster
gangplank

gangway
gap-toothed
garam masala
garden-variety (adj)
gas-guzzler
gatehouse
gatekeeper
gateway
gearshift
gee-whiz
gefilte fish
gemstone
Generation X
Generation Xer
Gen X
Gen Xer
geoduck
German shepherd
German shorthaired pointer
German wirehaired pointer
germ cell
germfree
gesundheit
getaway (n)
get-go (n)
get-together (n)
get-up-and-go (n)
g-force
giant schnauzer
ginkgo biloba
ginseng
give-and-take (n, adj)
giveaway (n)
glasshouse
glassware
glassy-eyed
globe-trotter
go-ahead (n)
goalkeeper
goal line

goalpost
gobbledygook
go-between (n)
god-awful (adj)
godforsaken
Godspeed
gofer
go-getter (n)
gold digger
golden retriever
goldenrod
goldfish
gold mine
Golf (communications code for G)
good-for-nothing (n, adj)
good-hearted
good-humored
good-looking (adj)
good-natured (adj)
goodwill
Goody Two-Shoes (n)
goody-two-shoes (adj)
goof-off (n)
Google Earth ™
googly-eyed
goose bumps
goose egg
gooseneck
Gorgonzola cheese
go-round (n)
go-to (adj)
Gouda cheese
goy
goyim
gram-negative
gram-positive
grandaunt
grandbaby
grandchild
granddad

granddaddy
granddaughter
grandfather
grandkid
grand mal seizure
grandmother
grandnephew
grandniece
grandpa
grandparent
grandson
grandstand
granduncle
Granny Smith apple
grasshopper
grassroots (adj)
G-rated
Graves' disease
graveside
gravestone
graveyard
great-aunt
Great Dane
great-nephew
great-niece
great-uncle
greenhouse
greenkeeper
greenroom
greyhound (dog)
Greyhound ™
gridiron
gridlock
grindstone
grittiness
groundbreaker
groundbreaking
ground crew
groundhog
groundskeeper

groundwater
grown-up (n, adj)
G-string
guardrail
guesstimate
guesswork
guesthouse
guidebook
gumbo-limbo
gumdrop
gumshoe
gunfight
gunfire
gung ho
gunmetal
gunpoint
gunpowder
gunshot
gun-shy
gunsmith

—H—

habeas corpus
habit-forming (adj)
hacksaw
hailstorm
hair ball
hairbrush
hairdresser
hairline
hairnet
hairpiece
hairpin
hairstyle
hairstylist
hairy-chested
half-and-half (n)
half-assed
halfback
half-baked

half-court (n)
half-dollar
halfhearted
half-mast (n, v)
half-moon
half nelson
half-pint (n, adj)
half-pipe (n)
half shell
half-staff
halftime (n)
half-time (adj)
half-truth
halfway
halfway house
half-wit
hallmark
hammerhead
hammertoe
hamstring
handbag
handball
handbasket
handblown
handbook
handcuff
hand-feed
handheld
hand-holding
hand in glove
hand in hand
handlebar
handmade
hand-me-down
handout (n)
hand over fist
handpick
handpress
handprint
hand sanitizer

handshake
hands-on (adj)
hand towel
handwrite
handyman
hang glide
hang glider
hang gliding
hangnail
hang-up (n)
hanky-panky
haphazard
happy-go-lucky
harbormaster
harborside
hardback
hard-boil
hard-boiled
hard copy
hard-core
hardcover
hard disk
hard drive
hardheaded
hard-hearted
hard-hit
hard knocks
hardnose
hard-nosed
hard-pressed
hardtop
hardware
harebrained
hash browns
hashtag
hatchback
hatha yoga
hay fever
hayride
haywire

hazmat
headache
headband
headboard
headcheese
head count (also headcount)
headfirst
headhunter
head-hunting
head-in-the-sand (adj)
headlight
headline
headmaster
headnote
head-on (adv, adj)
headphone
headstand
headstone
headstrong
heads-up (n, adj)
head-to-head (adj, adv)
headwaiter
headway
health care (healthcare)
hearsay
heartache
heartbeat
heartbreak
heartbroken
heartburn
heartfelt
heart-healthy (adj)
heart-lung machine
heart-stopping
heartthrob
heart-to-heart (adj, n)
heartwarming
heatstroke
heat wave
heave-ho

heaven-sent
heavyset
hedgehog
heebie-jeebies
Heimlich maneuver
helipad
heliport
henceforth
henpeck
hepatitis A
hepatitis B
hepatitis C
hereafter
hereinabove
hereinafter
hereinbefore
hereinbelow
hereof
hereon
herpesvirus
herpes zoster
herringbone
high-and-mighty
high-class (adj)
high-end
highfalutin
high-pitched (adj)
high-powered (adj)
high-pressure (adj)
high-rise (adj)
hijack (or high-jack)
hightail
high tide
high-top
high-voltage (adj)
hillbilly
hilltop
hindsight
HIPAA (Health Insurance Portability and Accountability Act)
hip-hop

hirsute
hitchhike
hitchhiker
hit-or-miss (adj)
hodgepodge
Hodgkin's disease
hoity-toity
hokey-pokey
holdback (n)
hole in one (hole-in-one, golf)
hole-in-the-wall (n)
homebound
homegrown
homelike
homemade
homemaker
homeroom
homeschool
homesick
hometown (n)
Honda CR-V ™
Honda CR-Z ™
honeybee
honeycomb
honeydew
honeypot
hookup (n)
hors d'oeuvre
horseshoe
hot-blooded
Hotel (communications code for H)
hotheaded
hot key
hotshot
hot spot (hotspot)
hot tub
houndstooth
hourglass
houseguest
household

housekeeper
housekeeping
housepainter
house sitter
housewares
housewarming
housewife
howsoever
how-to (adj, n)
hubcap
Hula-Hoop
hunt-and-peck (n)
husky (dog)

—I—

ibid (law)
Ibizen hound
ibuprofen
ice bag
iceberg
iceboat
icebox
icebreaker
ice-cold (adj)
ice-cream (adj)
ice hockey
icehouse
icemaker
iceman
ice milk
ice pack
ice pick
ice-skate (v)
ice skate (n)
ice-skater
ice-skating
idiosyncrasy
idiot savant
I formation (football)
ill-advised

ill-being
ill-bred
illegible
ill-fated
ill-favored
ill-humored
ill-mannered
ill-natured
ill-tempered
ill-use
ill will
ill-wisher
immune response
immune system
immunoassay
immunocompromised
immunodeficiency
immunosuppression
immunotherapy
impugn
inartful (used often, not in dictionary)
inartfully (used often, not in dictionary)
inasmuch as
in-box (n)
inbred
inbreed
inbreeding
in camera
inchworm
indebted
indebtedness
India (communications code for I)
Indian giver
industrial-strength
indwell (v)
indwelling (adj)
infielder
infighting
inflammatory bowel disease
in-flight

inground
ingrown (adj)
in-house (adj)
inhuman
inkblot
inkblot test
in-kind (adj)
ink-jet (adj)
inkwell
inland
in-law
in-line (adj)
in-line skate
in loco parentis
inner city (n)
inner-city (adj)
innermost
inner tube
innkeeper
in personam
in propria persona
ins and outs
inseam
inside out
insider trading
inside track
insofar as
insomuch as
insomuch that
in-store (adj)
instant message (n, v)
instant messaging
insulin-dependent diabetes
inter-American
interbank
intercampus
intercaste
intercellular
interchange
interchannel

intercity (between cities)
intercoastal
intercourse
interdepartmental
interface
interlay
interleukin-1
interleukin-2
interlocutory
internuclear
intra-arterial
intra-articular
intracardiac
intracellular
intracerebral
intracranial
intramuscular
intranasal
intrathecal
intrauterine
intrinsic factor
in vitro fertilization
in-your-face (adj)
ipso facto
Irish setter
Irish terrier
Irish water spaniel
Irish wolfhound
ironclad
ironfisted
ironhearted
iron horse
iron lung
Italian greyhound
ivory tower (n)
ivory-tower (adj)
Ivy League

—J—

jabberwocky

jackhammer
jack-in-the-box
jackknife
jack-of-all-trades
jackpot
jackrabbit
Jack Russell terrier
Jacob's ladder
Jacuzzi
jailbait
jailbird
jailbreak
jailhouse
jambalaya
jarhead
jawbone
jawbreaker
jaw-dropping
jawline
jaybird
jazzman
jazz-rock
Jell-O
jelly bean (jellybean)
jellyfish
jelly roll
jerry-build
jerry-built
jerry-rigged
jet-black (adj)
jet lag
jetliner
jet-propelled
jet set (n)
jet-set (adj)
jet-setter (adj)
jet-setting (adj)
Jet Ski ™
jet stream
jewfish

jigsaw
Jimmy John's ™
jitterbug
job-hopper (n)
job-hopping (n)
jobless
Joe Blow
Johnny-come-lately
joie de vivre
Jos. A. Bank ™
journeyman
journeywork
joyride
joystick
JPEG (photo computer file)
Judeo-Christian
juggernaut
jujitsu (jiujitsu)
Juliett (communications code for J)
jump rope
jump seat
jumpsuit
june bug
junk bond
junk e-mail
junk food
junkyard
Juris Doctor
jurisprudence
justice of the peace
juvenile-onset diabetes
juxtapose

—K—

kaffeeklatsch
Kaffir lime
Kaposi's sarcoma
Kawasaki disease
keelboat
keepsake

Kegel exercises
kelly green
Keogh plan
Kerry blue terrier
kettledrum
keyboard
keyhole
keynote
keynote address
keynote speaker
keypad (often handheld keyboard)
key pad (pad on the key of a wind instrument)
keypunch (n, v)
keystroke
key word
kibitz
kibosh
kickback (n)
kick back (v)
kickboard
kickboxing
kickoff (n)
kick off (v)
kickstand
kick-start (v)
kick start (n)
kick-starter
kid-glove (adj)
kid glove (n)
killjoy
Kilo (communications code for K)
kilobyte
kilogram
kilohertz
kiloliter
kilometer
kilowatt
kilowatt-hour
King Charles spaniel
kingfish

kingfisher
king mackerel
kingpin
King's English
king-size
king-sized
king's ransom
kiss-and-tell (adj)
kiteboard
kiteboarding
kittycorner
kitty-cornered
kiwifruit
kneecap
knee-deep (adj)
knee-high (n, adj)
knee-jerk (adj)
knee jerk (n)
knee-slapper (n)
knickerbocker
knickknack (also nicknack)
knitwear
knock-down, drag-out (adj)
knock-down-drag-out (n)
knock-kneed
knockoff (n)
knock off (v)
knockout (adj)
knothole
know-how (n)
know-it-all (n, adj)
knuckleball
knucklebone
knucklehead
Kohl's ™
Komodo dragon
Krebs cycle
kvetch
kvitch

—L—

label maker (sometimes one word as brand name)
labor-intensive (adj)
labor-saving (adj)
labradoodle
Labrador retriever
laches (legal; delay in pursuing a right)
lackadaisical
lackluster
lacrosse
lacto-ovo vegetarian
la-di-da
ladybug
ladyfinger
lady-in-waiting
lady-killer
ladylike
laid-back (adj)
laissez-faire
lakefront
lakeshore
lakeside
la-la land
lambskin
lamplight
lamppost
landfall
landfill
landlord
landlubber
landmark
landmass
landscape
landslide
lap belt
lapboard
lapdog
laptop

largehearted
large-minded
largemouth bass
large-print (adj)
larger-than-life (adj)
LASIK (laser-assisted in situ keratomileusis)
last-ditch (adj)
latches (fasteners, not a lock)
latchkey
latchkey child
latecomer
laughingstock (n)
launchpad
Laundromat
law-abiding (adj)
law-and-order (adj)
lawbreaker
lawmaker
layaway
layman (often used, layman's terms)
layoff (n)
lay off (v)
layover (n)
lay over (v)
laypeople
layperson
layup (n)
lay up (v)
lazy eye
lazy Susan
leaderboard
lead-in (n)
leapfrog
leapfrogging
leap year
leasehold
leaseholder
leatherback
leeway
left-hand (adj)

left-handed
leftmost
leftover (n, adj)
left-sided
left-turn lane
Legionnaires' disease
LEGO ™
LEGOs ™
legwork
lemongrass
lengthways
lengthwise
letdown (n)
let down (v)
letterhead
letter-perfect (adj)
levelheaded
lickety-split
lienholder
life-and-death (adj)
lifeboat
life-care
life expectancy
life force
life-form
life-giving
lifeguard
life jacket
lifeless
lifelike
lifeline
lifelong
life of Riley
life-or-death (adj)
lifesaver
life-size
life span
lifestyle
life-support (adj)
life support

lifetime
life vest
lifework
liftgate
lightbulb
light-headed
lighthearted
light heavyweight
lighthouse
light show
lights-out (n)
lightweight
light-year
likewise
lily-white (n, adj)
Lima (communications code for L)
lime-juicer (n)
limelight
limestone
limited-access (adj)
limited edition (n)
linchpin (preferred; also lynchpin)
linebacker
line-item (adj)
line item (n)
lineup (police lineup)
LinkedIn ™
lion's den
lion's share
lip-lock (n)
lip-read (v)
lip-reader
lip-reading (v)
lipreading (n)
lipstick
lip-sync (v)
lip sync (n)
LISTSERV
litterbug
Little League

live-bearer (n)
live-in (adj)
live in (v)
livelong
livestock
living room
lo and behold
loathesome
lockbox
lockdown (n)
locker-room (adj)
locker room (n)
lockjaw
lockout (n)
lock out (v)
logbook
loggerhead
log in (v)
login (n)
long-distance (adv)
long distance (n)
long-drawn-out (adj)
longhand
longhorn
long johns
longneck
long-range
long shot (n)
long-standing
long-suffering
long-term (adj)
longtime
long-winded
look-alike (n)
looking glass
lookout (n)
look out (v)
look-see
loophole
loosey-goosey

lose-lose (adj)
loudmouth
loudmouthed
loudspeaker
Lou Gehrig's disease
lovemaking
loveseat
lovesick
lovey-dovey
loving-kindness
lowdown (the facts)
low-down (adj, deeply emotional)
low-end (adj)
lowercase
lower-class (adj)
lower class (n)
lowermost
low-grade
low-key
low-keyed
low-level
lowlife
lowlight
low-lying
low-pressure (adj)
low-rise (adj)
low-spirited (adj)
low-tech (adj)
lukewarm
lumberjack
lumberman
lumberyard
lunchroom
lupus erythematosus
Lyme disease
lymph gland
lymph node

—M—

machinelike
Macy's
mad cow disease
made-to-order (adj)
made-up (adj)
madhouse
madman
madwoman
Magic Marker
magna cum laude
magnum opus
magpie
mahimahi
mahjong
mailbox
mail carrier
mail drop
mailman
mail order
Maine coon
mainframe
mainland
mainstay
mainstream
mai tai
maitre d'
maitre d's
major-medical (adj)
make-believe (n, adj)
make-do (n, adj)
make-or-break (adj)
makeover (n)
makeshift (n, adj)
makeup (n)
mako shark
male-pattern baldness
malfeasance

malingerer
Maltese (dog)
malware
Manchester terrier
man-eater (n)
manhandle
Manhattan (cocktail)
manhood
man-hours
manhunt
manic-depressive
mani-pedi (industry term)
mankind
manlift
man-made (adj)
man-of-war
manpower
manslaughter
man's man
manta ray
mantelpiece
man-to-man
Mardi Gras
markdown (n)
mark down (v)
marketplace
market share
marksman
markup (n)
mark up (v)
mason jar
mass-market (adj)
mass-produce (v)
master in science (uncap the specialty)
mastermind
Master of Science (cap the specialty)
masterpiece
master plan
master's degree
master's in science (uncap the specialty)

master's of science (uncap the specialty)
masthead
mastiff
matchbook
matchbox
matchmaker
match play
match point
matchstick
matchup (n)
matter-of-fact (adj)
matzo ball
maxillofacial
Mayday (distress call)
maypole
Mazda CX-5
Mazda CX-9
Mazda MX-5 Miata
mazel tov
McDonald's ™
meadowland
meals-on-wheels
meal ticket
mealtime
mealworm
meaningful
meaningless
mean-spirited
meantime
meanwhile
meat-and-potatoes (adj)
meat and potatoes (n)
meathead
meat loaf
meatpacking
MEd (Master of Education)
meddlesome
medevac (medical evacuation)
medevacked (past tense of medevac)
medicolegal (sounds like medical/legal)

meet and greet (n)
megabyte
megaphone
megapixel
megastar
megatonnage
megillah (slang, "the whole megillah")
Megillah (Judaism, scroll of Esther)
melodramatic
melting pot
meme (to imitate)
Ménière's disease
menorah
mens rea
menswear
mentsh
menu-driven (adj)
Mercedes-Benz ™
merchant marine
merry-go-round
meshiekh
meshugene
meshugener
metadata
metallurgy
metalsmith
metalware
metalwork
metalworking
meter maid
meterstick
MetroPCS ™
metrosexual
microbiology
microblogging
microbrewery
microchip
microfiber
microfiche
micromanage

microphone
microprocessor
microscope
microsurgery
microwave
midair
Midas touch
midbrain
middle-aged
Middle America
middle-American (adj)
Middle American (n)
middle-class (adj)
middle class (n)
middle ground
middleman
middle management
middle name
middle-of-the-road (adj)
middleweight
middorsal
midfield
midfielder
midlife
midlife crisis
midline
midnight
midpoint
midrib
midriff
midsagittal
midsection
midsize
midstream
midsummer
midterm
midway
midweek
midwife
midwifery

midwinter
midyear
Mike (communications code for M)
milepost
milestone
milk shake
millpond
millstone
millwork
mimic
mimicking
mincemeat
mind-altering
mind-bending
mind-blowing
mind-boggling
mind-numbing
mind reader
mind-set
mind's eye
minefield
miniature pinscher
miniature schnauzer
minibar
minibike
minidress
mini-mart
miniseries
miniskirt
ministroke
minitower
minivan
Minnesota Multiphasic Personality Inventory (MMPI)
minuteman
Miranda rights
Miranda warning
Mirandize
misadjust
misalign
misassemble

misbehave
miscarriage
miscarry
mischievous
misconceive
misconception
misconstrue
misdiagnose
misdial
misfile
misfire
misfortune
misfunction
misgiving
mishap
mishmash
misinterpret
mislabel
mislead
mislocate
mismanage
mismark
mismatch
misprint
misquote
misshape
misshapen
misspeak
misspell
misspelling
misspoke
misstate
misstep
mistranslate
mistruth
misty-eyed
mistype
miter box
mixed martial arts
mixed-use (adj)

mix-up (n)
mobile home
mockingbird
modus operandi
Mohs' scale
mom-and-pop (adj)
Monday-morning quarterback
Monday-morning quarterbacking
money-back (adj)
moneybags
MoneyGram ™
money-grubber
moneygrubbing
moneylender
moneymaker
moneyman
money market
money order
monkey wrench
monofilament
Monterey Jack
Montezuma's revenge
monthlong
mood disorder
moonbeam
moondust
moonfaced
moonfish
moonlight
moonlit
moonrise
moonscape
moonshine
moonstruck
moonwalk
moreover
morning-after pill
Morse code
mosh pit
mosslike

moss-grown
mothball
moth-eaten
motherboard
mother-of-pearl (n)
mother ship
motorbike
motorboat
motorboater
motorboating
motorcade
motorcar
motorcycle
motor home
motormouth
motormouthed
motor vehicle
motorway
mountainside
Mountain time
mountaintop
mouse pad
mousetrap
mouthfeel
mouthful
mouthpiece
mouth-to-mouth (adj)
mouthwash
mouthwatering
moviegoer
moviegoing
moviemaker
moviemaking
MRSA (methicillin-resistant staphylococcus aureus)
muckety-muck
mud flap
mudguard
mudroom
mudslinger
mudslinging (n, name-calling)

multiagency
multiaxial
multicar
multichambered
multichannel
multicity
multidimensional
multidirectional
multifaceted
multifactorial
multifunctional
multigrain
multi-industry
multi-institutional
multilayered
multilevel
multimedia
multimember
multipage
multipart
multiparty
multiphasic
multiplayer
multiple-choice (adj)
multiple personality disorder
multipurpose
multiregional
multisyllabic
multitasking
multivitamin
multivoiced
mumbo jumbo
Munchausen syndrome
Munchausen syndrome by proxy
Murphy bed
Murphy's Law
muscle-bound
muscle car
muscleman
muscle shirt

Muscovy duck
muscular dystrophy
museumgoer
must-have (n)
must-see (n)
muttonchops
muttonfish
myotonic dystrophy

—N—

nail bed
nail-biter (n)
nailbrush
nail file
naivete
naked mole rat
namby-pamby (n, adj)
name-calling (n)
name-dropping (n)
nameless
nameplate
namesake
nannoplankton
nanoparticle
nanosecond
nanotechnology
nanotube
Napa cabbage
napoleon (dessert)
narrow-minded (adj)
narrow-mindedly (adv)
narrow-mindedness (n)
narwhal
nasogastric
nasopharyngeal
nasopharynx
National Guard
national guard (outside the US)
National Guardsman
nationwide

Native American
natural gas
Naugahyde ™
naysayer
Neapolitan ice cream
near-infrared (adj)
near miss (n)
nearsighted
nearsightedly
nearsightedness
neatnik
neck and neck (adv, adj)
necktie
necrotizing fasciitis
needle-nose pliers
needlepoint
needlework
ne'er-do-well (n)
neocortex
neo-Darwinian
neo-Expressionism
neo-Freudian
neo-impressionism
neonatal
neonate
neonatology
neo-Nazi
neoorthodox
neo-pagan
nerve-racking (also nerve-wracking)
nervous breakdown
nest egg
netbook
neuroimaging
neuromuscular
neuropathology
neuropharmacology
neuropsychiatry
neuropsychology
neuroradiology

neuroscience
neurosecretion
neurosensory
neurosurgery
neurotransmission
neurotransmitter
never mind
never-never land
nevertheless
new age
newborn
newfangled
new-fashioned (adj)
newfound (adj)
Newfoundland (dog)
new jack swing
newlywed
newsbreak
newscast
newsdealer
newsgroup
newsletter
newsmagazine
newsman
newsmonger
newspaperman
newspaperwoman
newspeak
newspeople
newsperson
newsprint
newsreader
newsreel
newsroom
newsstand
newsweekly
newswire
newswoman
newsworthy
newswriting

Newton's first law
Newton's second law
Newton's third law
new wave
New World
New York minute
next-door (adj)
next door (n)
next of kin
nickel-and-dime (adj, v)
nickel-and-dimed
nickel-and-diming
nickeled-and-dimed
nickeling-and-diming
nicknack (also knickknack)
nickname
night and day (adv)
night blindness
night-blooming jasmine (n)
nightcap
nightclothes
nightclub
night court
night crawler
nightdress
nightfall
nightglow
nightgown
nighthawk
nightingale
nightlife
night-light
nightlong (adj, adv)
nightmare
night owl
night rider
night shift
nightshirt
nightspot
nightstand

nightstick
night sweats
night table
nighttime
nightwalker
night watchman
nincompoop
ninespin
nine-to-fiver (n)
nitpick
nitpicker
nit-picking
nitpicky
nitty-gritty
nitwit
Nissan Xterra
Nobel Prize
nobleman
no-brainer
nociceptor
no-fault (adj)
no-frills (adj)
no-go (adj)
no-good (n, adj)
no-goodnik
no-holds-barred (adj)
nohow
noisemaker
nolle prosequi
nolo contendere
nol-prossed
nol-prossing
no-man's-land (n)
nomenclature
non-A hepatitis
non-American
non-B hepatitis
nonchalant
non compos mentis
nonfeasance

nonflammable
non-Hodgkin's lymphoma
non-insulin-dependent diabetes
non-insulin-dependent diabetes mellitus
no-nonsense
nonperforming
nonprofit
nonrecombinant
nonrefundable
nonresident
nonreturnable
non sequitur
nonskid
nonstick
nonstop
nonthreatening
noontime
no-par-value
nor'easter (storm)
Norfolk terrier
north (referring to directions)
North (referring to regions; i.e., North Texas)
Northerner (one who lives in the North)
Northern Hemisphere
northern lights
northernmost
north-northeast
north-northwest
North Pole
North Star
northwest
Northwesterner
Norwegian elkound
Norwich terrier
nosebleed
nosedive
no-see-um
noseguard
Nosey Parker
no-show (n, adj)

notepad
notepaper
note-taking
noteworthy
not-for-profit (adj)
nother (adj)
notwithstanding
nouveau riche
November (communications code for N)
Novocain ™
novocaine
nowadays
nowhere
nowheres
no-win (adj)
nth degree
nth time
numbskull
nursemaid
nurse-midwife
nurse-practitioner
nurse's aide
nursing home
nutcase
nutcracker
nuthouse
nutmeg
nutshell
Nuyorican

—O—

ob-gyn (physician)
OB-GYN (specialty, commonly OB/GYN)
obssessive-compulsive (adj)
Occam's razor
occipital bone
occipital lobe
occiput
oddball
odd man out

odds and ends
offbeat
off-brand (adj)
off Broadway (n)
off-Broadway (adj)
off-color (adj)
off-grounds
offhand (adv)
offhanded (adj)
officeholder
off-key (adj, adv)
off-kilter (adj)
off-limits (adj)
off-line (adj)
off-load (v)
off-off-Broadway (n, adj, adv)
off-peak (adj)
off-putting (adj)
off-ramp (n)
off-road (adj)
off-roader (n)
off-scene
off-season (n)
offset
offshoot
offshore (adv, adj, prep)
offside (adv, adj)
off-site (adj, adv)
offspring
offstage (adv, adj)
off-the-books (adj)
off the books (adv)
off-the-cuff (adj, adv)
off-the-rack (adj)
off-the-record (adj)
off-the-wall (adj)
offtrack (adv, adj)
off-white (n)
oftentimes
ohm

Ohm's law
oilcan
oil field
oilman
oil paint
oil pan
oil well
okeydoke
okeydokey
old adage
Old English sheepdog
oldfangled
old-fashioned (adj, n)
old-school (adj)
Old Testament
old-time (adj)
old-timer (n)
olfactory nerve
Olympian
Olympic
Olympic Games
ombudsman
omega-3
omnibus
omnidirectional
omnipotent
on-again, off-again (adj)
on and off (adv)
on-and-off (adj)
onboard (adj)
once-over (n)
one-armed bandit
one-dimensional (adj)
onefold
one-handed (adj)
one-liner (n)
one-man band
one-nighter
one-night stand
one-on-one (adj, adv)

one-piece (adj, n)
oneself
one-sided (adj)
one-sidedness (n)
one-size-fits-all (adj)
one-stop (adj)
onetime (adj)
one-to-one (adj)
one-track (adj)
one-trick pony
one-two punch
one-way (adj)
ongoing
on-grounds
onionskin
onlooker
onlooking
on-ramp (n)
on-scene (adj, adv)
on-screen
onset (n)
on-site (adj, adv)
onstage (adj, adv)
on-target (adj)
on-the-job (adj)
onto (adj)
oomph
open-air (adj)
open-and-shut (adj)
open-door (adj)
open-end (adj)
open-ended (adj)
open enrollment
open-eyed (adj)
open-faced (adj)
openhanded (adj)
openhandedly
openhandedness
open-heart (adj)
openhearted (adj)

openheartedly
openheartedness
open house
open-minded (adj)
open-mindedly
open-mindedness
openmouthed
openmouthedly
openmouthedness
optic cup
optic disk
optic lobe
optic nerve
Oriental rug
O-ring
Oscar (communications code for O)
osso buco
osteosarcoma
otitis media
ottoman (footrest)
out-and-out (adj)
outback
outboard (adj, adv, n)
outbreak
outcast (n, adj)
outcome
outcry
outdated
outdo
outdoor
outdoorsman
outdoorsy
outermost
outerwear
outfield
outfit
outfitter
outflow (n, v)
outfox (v)
outgoing

outgrew
outgrow
outgrown
outgrowth
outguess
outhouse
outlandish
outlandishly
outlandishness
outlay (v, n)
outline (n, v)
outlive
outlook
outlying
outmost
outnumber
out-of-body (adj)
out-of-bounds (adv, adj)
out-of-date (adj)
out-of-doors (adj)
out-of-pocket (adj)
out-of-sight (adj)
out-of-the-way (adj)
outpace
outparcel
outpatient
outplacement
outpost
outpour (v, n)
outpouring (n)
output
outrace
outrage
outrank
outreach (v, n)
outrigger
outright (adv, adj)
outrun
outsell
outset

outshine
outsider
outskirt (n)
outslick
outsmart
outsole
outsource
outspoken
outspokenly
outspokenness
outstanding
outtake
out-there (adj)
outward
outward-bound
outwardly
outweigh
outwit
Oval Office
ovenproof
overachiever
overact
overactive
overactivity
overaged (adj)
overall
over and above
overbear
overbearing
overbite
overboard (adv)
overcast
overcoat
overcome
overdo
overdose
overdraft
overdraw
overdrawn
overdress

overdue
overeat
overexpose
overextend
overfeed
overfill
overflow
overgrow
overgrown
overhand
overhaul
overhead
overhear
overheat
overheated
overjoyed
overkill
overlap
overlay
overnight
overpass
overpopulate
overpower
overprice
overqualified
overreach
override
overripe
overrule
overrun
overseas
oversee
overseer
overshadow
overshirt
overshoot
oversight
oversimplify
oversize
oversleep

overslept
overspend
overspray
overstay
overstuff
overtake
over-the-counter (adj)
over-the-hill (adj)
over-the-top (adj)
overthrow
overtime (n)
overtone
overturn
overweight
overwhelm
overwhelmingly
over with
overwork
overwrite
ovo-lacto vegetarian
oxbow
oxtail
oxymoron
oysters Rockefeller
ozone layer
ozonosphere

—P—

pace car
pacemaker
pacesetter
pachyderm
Pacific time
packinghouse
pack journalism
pack rat
paddleboard
paddleboat
paddy wagon
pad thai

Paget's disease
page-turner
painkiller
painstaking
paintball
paintbrush
Pandora's box
panfry
panhandle
panic attack
panic disorder
panicked
panicking
panic-stricken
pantsuit
panty hose
Papa (communications code for P)
Papanicolaou smear
Papanicolaou test
paperboy
paper clip
papermaker
paper-thin (adj)
paper trail
paperweight
paperwork
papier mâché
Pap smear
parajournalism
Paralympian
Paralympics
paramilitary
paranoid schizophrenia
paranormal
paraprofessional
parasailing
parasympathetic
paratrooper
parcel post
Parent-Teacher Association

paresthesia
pari-mutuel
parkinsonian
parkinsonism
Parkinson's disease
Parkinson's Law
parkway
Parmesan cheese
parotid gland
parrot fish
partake
part and parcel (n)
particleboard
part-time (always)
party animal
partyer
partygoer
party pooper
passageway
passerby
passersby
passionflower
passion fruit
passive-aggressive (adj, n)
passkey
passport
pass-through (n)
password
pastime
patchwork
patent leather
patent office
pathway
patron saint
patty-cake (or pat-a-cake)
Pavlovian
pawnbroker
pawnshop
pay-as-you-go (adj)
payback (n)

paycheck
payday
payload
paymaster
payoff (n, adj, v)
payout (n)
pay-per-view (n)
pay phone
payroll
pay stub
pay-TV (n)
peace corps
peacekeeping
peacekeeper
peacemaker
peace offering
peace officer
peacetime
peachy keen
peacoat
peacock
peak flow meter
pear-shaped
peat moss
pedal pushers
peekaboo
peephole
Peeping Tom
peep show
peer review (n)
peer-review (v)
Peg-Board ™
peg leg
Peking duck
Pekingese (dog, or Pekinese)
pencil pusher
penholder
penknife
penknives
penmanship

penny-ante (adj)
penny ante (n)
penny-pinching
pennyweight
penny-wise and pound-foolish
pen pusher
people mover
peppercorn
pepper mill
pepper spray
Pepsi-Cola ™
pep talk
perception-reaction time (industry term)
per diem
peremptory challenge
per se
Persian cat
persnickety
person of interest
per stirpes
petit four
petit jury
petit larceny
petit mal
PET scan
PET scanner
PET scanning
petty officer
petty officer first class
petty officer second class
petty officer third class
PharmD (Doctor of Pharmacy)
phaseout (n)
phase out (v)
PhD (Doctor of Philosophy)
Phi Beta Kappa
Phillips screwdriver
phishing (e-mail scam)
phosphoprotein
photocopy

photo-essay
photo finish
photofinisher
photograph
photoinduced
photojournalism
photokinesis
photomontage
photophobia
photoreceptor
Photoshop ™ (the brand and the verb)
phototypesetting
phytonutrient
picket line
picklock
pick-me-up (n)
pickpocket
pickup (adj, n)
pick up (v)
picnicked
picnicking
picture-perfect (adj)
piecemeal (n, adv, adj)
piecrust
pie-faced (adj)
piehole
pie-in-the-sky (adj)
Pier 1 Imports ™
pigeonhole (n, v)
pigeon-toed
piggyback
piggy bank
pigheaded
pig Latin
pig out (v)
pig-out (n)
pigpen
pigskin
pigtail
pigtailed

Pilates
pillbox
pillowcase
pillow talk
pilothouse
PIN (personal identification number)
pinball
pinch-hit (v)
pinch hit (n)
pinch hitter
pinchpenny (adj)
pincushion
pineapple
pinecone
ping-pong (v, going back and forth)
Ping-Pong ™ (n, table tennis)
pinhead (n)
pinhole
pink slip
pinpoint
pinprick
pint-size (adj)
pint-sized (adj)
pinwheel
pipe fitter
pipe fitting
pipe layer
pip-squeak
pistol-whip (v)
pit bull
pit bull terrier
pitch-black (adj)
pitch-dark (adj)
pitchfork
pitch-perfect (adj)
pit stop
pitter-patter (n)
placebo effect
placeholder
place mat

plainclothes
plain-Jane (adj)
plain Jane (n)
plain-laid
plan B
Planck's constant
plasterboard
plasterwork
plasticware
plate glass (n)
platelet
platinum blonde
playback (n)
play back (v)
playbill (bill advertising a play)
Playbill ™ (theater program)
playbook
play-by-play (n, adj)
playdate
playground
playgroup
playhouse
playoffs (sports)
playpen
playroom
playtime
playwright
playwriting
Plexiglas ™
plexiglass
plowshare
plug and play (n)
plug-and-play (adj)
plug-in (n, adj)
plug in (v)
plus/minus sign
pneumothorax
pocketbook
pocketknife
pocketknives

pocket money
pocket-sized
pockmark
podcast
podcaster
pogo stick
point-and-click (adj)
point-and-shoot (adj)
point-blank (adj)
point-of-purchase (adj)
poker face
policyholder
poliovirus
polka dot (n)
polka-dot (adj)
polka-dotted (adj)
polycystic kidney disease
polycystic ovary syndrome
polyethylene glycol
polymerase chain reaction
polynuclear
polypeptide
polyphenol
polypropylene
polyrhythm
polytechnic
Pomeranian
pom-pom
ponytail
Ponzi scheme
poodle
pooh-bah
poolside
pooper-scooper
pop quiz
Popsicle ™
pop-top (n)
pop-up (n, adj)
pork belly
portal-to-portal (adj)

porterhouse
porthole
posterior cruciate ligament (PCL)
postgrad
postgraduate
Postimpressionism
Postimpressionist
Post-It ™
postman
postmark
postmaster
postmaster general
postmenopausal
postmodern
postmortem
postmortem examination
postnasal drip
postnuptial
post-op (adj, adv)
postoperative
postpartum
postprandial
postscript
postsurgical
post-traumatic stress disorder
posturing
potbellied pig
potbellied stove
potbelly
pot cheese
potluck
potpourri
pot roast
pot sticker
potty-mouthed
pound sign
poverty line
poverty-stricken
powerboat
power-dive (v)

power dive (n)
powerhouse
powerless
power of attorney
power play
power steering
power strip
power train
power up (v)
power-up (n)
power walk
powwow (n, v)
poxvirus
Prader-Willi syndrome
prairie dog
praiseworthy
prayerful
prayer meeting
praying mantis
precancerous
precast
pre-Christian
pre-Columbian
preconceive
precondition
precook
prediabetes
predispose
preeclampsia
preemergence
preemergent
preemie (premie)
preeminence
preeminent
preempt
preemption
preemptive
pre-engineered
preexist
preexistence

preexisting
prefab
prefabricate
preferred provider organization (PPO)
preflight
prefrontal cortex
preganglionic
pre-Hispanic
prejudge
pre-K
prekindergarten
premalignant
premed
premeditate
premenstrual dysphoric disorder
premenstrual syndrome
premolar
prenuptial
prenuptial agreement
pre-op
preoperative
pre-owned
prepackaged
prepay
Pre-Raphaelite
prerogative
present-day (adj)
pre-Socratic
pressboard
press box
press conference
press kit
pressman
pressmark
pressroom
press secretary
pressure cooker
pressure-cook
presswork
preteen-ager

price-cutter (n)
price-fixing (n)
price index
price tag
prima facie
primrose
Prince Charming
Prince of Wales
printing office
printing press
printmaking
printout (n)
print out (v)
prisoner of war
private detective
private eye
private first class
private investigator
privilege
prizefighting
prizewinner
prizewinning
pro bono
pro-choice
pro-choicer
prodigy
profit and loss (n)
profiterole
pro forma
promissory note
proofreader
propeller-head
Proper (i.e., Boston Proper)
propranolol
pro rata
pro se (represent oneself)
prosecco
prostaglandin
prostate-specific antigen (PSA)
protein kinase C

proteinuria
prothrombin
prothrombin time
proudhearted
p's and q's
psychoanalyze
psychobabble
psychokinesis
psychology
psychoneuroimmunology
psychoneurosis
psychopath
psychopathic personality disorder
psychopharmacology
psychosocial
psychosomatic
psychosurgery
psychotherapeutic
psychotherapist
psychotherapy
psychotropic
psych-out (n)
psych out (v)
pterodactyl
pterygoid
pterygoid process
ptoses (plural)
ptosis
public-address system
puddle jumper
pull-down (adj)
pull down (v)
pullout (n)
pull out (v)
pullover (n)
pull over (v)
pull-up (n)
pull up (v)
pulse-jet engine
pumpernickel

punch bowl
punch-drunk (adj)
punch line
punch list
punch-out (n)
punch out (v)
pundit
punitive damages
puppy dog
puppy mill
pure-blooded
purebred
Purple Heart
purview
push broom
push-button (adj)
push button (n)
pushcart
pushdown (n)
push down (v)
pushover (n)
push over (v)
pushpin
push-pull (n, adj)
pushrod
push-up (n)
push up (v)
pussycat
pussyfoot
pussy willow
put-down (n)
put down (v)
putt-putt (n)
putty knife
put-upon (adj)
pyelonephritis
pyromania
pyrotechnic

—Q—

quaalude
quadratic equation
quadrilateral
quadruplicate
quahog
quality assurance
quarrelsome
quarterback
quarter binding
quarter-bound
quarterdeck
quarterfinal
quarter horse
quarter hour
quartermaster
quasi-governmental
quasi-judicial
quasi-legislative
quasi-public
quay
quayside
queasy
Quebec (communications code for Q)
queen-size
quenelle
quesadilla
quick bread
quick fix
quick-freeze (v)
quicksilver (n)
quickstep (n)
quick-tempered (adj)
quick-witted (adj)
quid pro quo
quinolone
quitclaim (n, v)
quitclaim deed

quitclaimed
quitclaiming
quixotic
quizzical
quorum
quote-unquote (surround with commas)

—R—

RaceTrac ™
rabbet joint
rabbit hole
rabble-rouser
raccoon
racecourse
racehorse
racemate
race runner
racetrack
racewalk
racewalker
racewalking
rack and pinion (n)
rack-and-pinion (adj)
racquetball
radial keratotomy
radiculopathy
radioactive
radiocarbon
radio frequency
radiography
radioisotope
radiosensitive
radio wave
ragtime
ragtop
rah-rah
railcar
railroad
railroading

railway
rainbow fish
rainbow trout
raincoat
rain date
raindrop
rainfall
rain forest
rainmaker
rain out (v)
rainout (n)
rainproof
rainspout
rainsquall
rainstorm
rain tree
rainwater
rainy day (n)
rainy-day (adj)
ranch house
ranchman
random-access memory
rapid eye movement
rapid-fire (adj)
ratatouille
rate of exchange
ratepayer
rattlesnake
rattrap
raucous (adj, disagreeably harsh)
raw bar
rawhide
razorback
razor-backed
razorbill
razzmatazz
reabsorption
reacquaint
reacquire
reactivate

readdress
readjust
read-only memory
ready-made
ready-to-wear
reaffirm
real time (n)
real-time (adj)
Realtor (collective mark)
real-world (adj)
reappear
rear end (n)
rear-end (v)
rear-ended
rear-ender (n)
rearview mirror
rearward
reassess
reattempt
reboil
reboot
recalculate
recede
recidivism
recidivist
recoil
recollect (remember)
re-collect (to collect again)
recombinant DNA
reconfigure
reconnect
recordkeeping
red-blooded
Red Delicious apples
redesign
redevelop
red-eye (n)
redeye gravy
red-handed
redhead

red herring
red-hot (adj)
red hot (n)
redial
redirect
redline
redneck
reelect
reel-to-reel
reemerge
reenact
reenergize
reenlist
reenroll
reequip
reestablish
reexamine
referee
referendum
reflexology
refreeze
refrigerator
regress
Reiki
reincarnate
reinvest
reinvestigate
Reiter's syndrome
relativistic
relief pitcher
remittitur
REM sleep
remunerate (v, to compensate monetarily)
Renaissance man
rendezvous
renege
reneged
reneging
renowned
rent-a-car

rent-a-cop
renumerate (v, to renumber)
repertoire
repertory
repugn
repugnance
repugnant
resection
restless legs syndrome
restraining order
restroom
resveratrol
retinitis pigmentosa
retinoblastoma
retinopathy
retriever (dog)
retroactive
retrofit
retrograde
Reuben sandwich
reuptake inhibitor
rev
reverse discrimination
reverse mortgage
reverse osmosis
revolving-door (adj)
revved
revving
Reye's syndrome
rhabdomyosarcoma
rhabdovirus
rhetoric
rhetorical
rheumatic fever
rheumatoid arthritis
Rh factor
rhinestone
rhinoplasty
rhinoscopy
rhinovirus

rhizome
Rhodesian ridgeback
Rhodes scholar
Rh-positive
rhubarb
rhyme or reason
rib cage
rib eye
riboflavin
ribosomal RNA
Richter scale
rickshaw
ridgeline
ridgetop
Riesling
rifleman
riffraff
rigamarole
right angle (n)
right-angle (adj)
right hand (n)
right-hand (adj)
right-handed
right-minded
rightmost (adj)
right-of-way (n)
right-sided
right-turn lane
right wing (n)
right-wing (adj)
right-winged
rigor mortis
ring-around-the-rosy
ringleader
ringmaster
ringside
ringtone
ringworm
rinky-dink
riparian rights

rip-off (n)
rip off (v)
rip-roaring
riptide
Rip van Winkle
Ritalin
rite of passage
ritzy
riverbank
riverbed
riverboat
riverfront
riverside
RNA polymerase
RNA virus
roadblock
road hog
roadhouse
roadkill
road map
road racing
road rage
road rash
roadrunner
road show
roadside
road test
road trip
road warrior
roadway
roadwork
roadworthy
robocall
rock-bottom (adj)
rockbottom (n)
rocker arm
rocking chair
rock lobster
rock 'n' roll
rock salt

rock shrimp
roentgen
roentgenography
role model
role-play (v)
rollback (n)
roll back (v)
roll bar (n)
roll cage
Rollerblade ™
roller-coaster (adj)
roller coaster (n)
roller rink
roller skate (n)
roller-skate (v)
roller skater (n)
rollout (n)
roll out (v)
rollover (n)
roll over (v)
rolltop desk
roly-poly
Roman numeral
Romeo (communications code for R)
roofline
rooftop
room and board
roommate
room service
rootkit (computers)
ropewalker
Roquefort cheese
Rorschach test
rosacea
rosebud
rosebush
rose-colored (adj)
rose hip
rosemary
rose oil

roseola
Rosetta stone (n)
Rosetta Stone ™
rosewater (adj)
rose water (n)
rosewood
Rosh Hashanah
rotary-wing aircraft
rotator cuff
rotavirus
rotisserie
rototill
rottweiler
rough-and-tumble (n, adj)
rough-edged
roughhouse (n, v)
roughneck
roughshod
round-shouldered
round-the-clock (adj)
round-trip (n)
roundup (n)
round up (v)
roundworm
rouseabout
Rous sarcoma
roustabout
roux
rowboat
row house
royal blue
royal flush
royal jelly
rubber band
rubber check
rubber-chicken (adj)
rubberneck (n, v)
rubbernecker
rubber-stamp (v)
rubber stamp (n)

rubdown (n)
rub down (v)
ruckus
rumrunner
runaway (n, adj)
run away (v)
rundown (n)
run-down (adj)
run down (v)
run in (v)
run-in (n)
runner-up
running back
running board
running mate
runoff (n)
run off (v)
run-of-the-mill
runover (n)
run-over (adj)
run over (v)
run-through (n)
run through (v)
runway
rupee
Russian roulette
Russian wolfhound
rustproof
rutabaga

—S—

sacroiliac
sacrosanct
sacrosanctity
saddlebag
saddle soap
saddle sore
safecracker
safecracking
safe-deposit box

safeguard
safe house
safekeeping
safe sex
safety-deposit box
sailboard
sailboarder
sailboarding
sailboat
sailfish
sailmaker
Saint Bernard
Saint-John's-wort
salesclerk
salesgirl
saleslady
salesman
salesmanship
salespeople
salesperson
salesroom
saleswoman
salicylic acid
Salisbury steak
sally port
saltshaker
saltwater
sandalwood
sandbag
sandbar
sandblast (n, v)
sandbox
sand-cast (v)
sand-casting (v)
sand casting (n)
sand dollar
sandglass
sandpaper
sandpit
sandshoe

sandsoap
sandstone
sandstorm
Sangiovese
Sanskrit
saucepan
sauvignon blanc
sawdust
sawed-off (adj)
sawhorse
sawmill
say-so (n)
scapegoat (n, v)
scarecrow
scaredy-cat (n)
scarlet fever
scarlet letter
scatterbrain
scatterbrained
scent hound
schizophrenia
schnauzer
school-age (adj)
schoolbag
schoolbook
schoolboy (n, adj)
school bus
schoolchild
school district
schoolgirl
schoolhouse
schoolmarm
schoolmaster
schoolmate
schoolroom
schoolteacher
schooltime
schoolwork
sciatic nerve
scissors hold (wrestling)

scissors kick (swimming)
scleroderma
scleroprotein
sclerotherapy
Scotch bonnet
Scotch terrier
scot-free
Scottie (Scottish terrier)
Scottish deerhound
Scottish Gaelic
Scottish rite
Scottish terrier
Scottrade ™
scoutmaster
screaming meemies
screenful
screenplay
screen saver
screenshot
screen test
screenwriter
screwball
screwdriver
screwup (n)
screw up (v)
scrub brush
scrub nurse
scuba
scuba dive
scuba diver
scuba diving
scuttlebutt
sea anemone
sea bass
seabed
seaboard (n, adj)
sea breeze
seacoast
seacraft
seafarer

seafood
sea grape
seagull
sea horse
sea lion
seaman
seamanlike
seamanship
sea otter
seaport
search engine
search warrant
sea rover
seascape
seashore
seasick
seasickness
seat belt
sea turtle
sea urchin
seawall
seaward
seawater
seaway
seaweed
seaworthiness
seaworthy
second-best (adj)
second best (n)
second-class (adj)
second class (n)
second-guess (v)
secondhand (adj, adv)
second hand (n)
secondhand smoke
second-rate (adj)
Second World
secretary-general (n)
Seeing Eye ™ dog
seersucker

seesaw
see-through
Segway
seismic
self-addressed
self-appointed
self-centered
self-fulfilling
self-help
selfhood
self-important
self-indulge
selfish
selfishness
selfless
selflessness
self-pity
self-publish
self-respect
selfsame
self-serving
self-supporting
self-worth
seller's market
sellout (n)
sell out (v)
semi (n, semidetached and short for semitrailer)
semi-antique
semiautomatic
semi-independent
semitrailer
semitruck
serendipity
sergeant first class
sergeant major
serious-minded
serology
seronegative
seropositive
serum hepatitis

service charge
service line
serviceman
service mark
service road
service station
setback (n)
setoff (n)
set off (v)
shakedown (n)
shake down (v)
shakeout (n)
shake out (v)
shake-up (n)
shake up (v)
Shangri-la
sharecropper
shareholder
shareware
sharkskin
shar-pei (dog)
sharp-eyed
sharpshooter
sharp-tongued
sharp-witted
shatterproof
she-crab
sheepdog
sheepherder
sheepshead
sheepskin
Sheetrock ™
shelf life
shellac
shellacked
shellacking
shellfish
shell shock
shell-shocked (adj)
sheltie (dog; also, shelty)

shenanigan
shepherd
shepherd's pie
Shetland pony
Shetland sheepdog
Shetland wool
shih tzu
Shiite
shinbone
shindig
shipbuilder
shipbuilding
shipfitter
shipload
shipmaster
shipmate
shipwreck
shipyard
Shiraz
shish kebab
shivah
shlep
shmeer
shmooz
shmuck
shnoz
shockproof
shock therapy
shock wave
shoehorn
shoelace
shoe-leather (adj)
shoemaker
shoestring
shogun
shoofly pie
shoo-in
shook-up (adj)
shoot-em-up (n)
shoot-out (n)

shopaholic
shopgirl
shopkeeper
shoplift
shoplifter
shoptalk
shorefront
shoreline
shore patrol
shoreside
shortcake
shortchange
short-circuit (v)
short circuit (n)
shortcoming
shortcut
shortfall
shorthand
shorthanded
short line
short-lived (adj)
short-order (adj)
short-range
short ribs
shortstop (n, baseball)
short-stop (n, stop bath)
short-tempered
short-term
short-winded
shotgun
shot put
shot-putter
shoulder blade
shoulder dystocia
shoulder girdle
shoulder strap
shout-out (n)
shout out (v)
show-and-tell (n)
showbiz

showboat (n, v)
showcase
showdown
showerhead
showgirl
show-me (adj)
show-off (n)
show off (v)
showpiece
showroom
showstopper
showtime
shrapnel
Shriner
shrinking violet
shrink-wrap
shtick
shuffleboard
shutdown (n)
shut down (v)
shut-eye (n)
shut-in (n, adj)
shut in (v)
shutoff (n)
shut off (v)
shutout (n)
shut out (v)
shyster
Siamese cat
Siamese twin
Siberian husky
sickbed
sick building syndrome
sick day
sickle cell
sickle-cell anemia
sickle-cell trait
sick pay
sickroom
sidearm

sidebar
sideburns
side by side (adv)
side-by-side (adj)
sidecar
side effect
side-glance
sidekick (n)
sideline (n, v)
side-scan sonar
sideshow
side-splitting (adj)
side step (n)
sidestep (v)
sidestepper
side street
sideswipe (v, n)
side table
sidetrack (n, v)
sideview (not in dictionaries; follows rearview)
sidewalk
sidewall
sideways
sidewinder
sidewise
sight hound
sightless
sightsee
sightseeing
sight unseen
Sierra (communications code for S)
sigmoid colon
sign off (v)
sign-off (n)
sign on (v)
sign-on (n)
sign out (v)
sign-out (adj)
silent partner
silent treatment

silk screen (n)
silk-screen (v)
silk-stocking (adj)
silk stocking (n)
silkworm
silky terrier
siltstone
silverback
silverfish
silver screen
silversmith
silver spoon
Silver Star (military medal)
silver-tongued (adj)
silverware
SIM card
simpleminded
simple sugar
simpleton
sing-along (n)
single-action (adj)
single-blind (adj)
single-handed (adj)
single-minded (adj)
single-space (v)
sinkhole
sinoatrial
sinoatrial node
sinus rhythm
siphon (syphon)
sisterhood
sister-in-law
sitcom
sit-down (n, adj)
sit-in (n)
sit in (v)
sitting duck
sitting room
sit-up (n)
sit up (v)

sitz bath
six-pack (n)
sixpence
sixpenny nail
six-shooter (n)
sixth sense
skateboard
skateboarder
SKECHERS ™
skedaddle
sketchbook
skid mark
skid row
ski jump
ski lift
skillful
skimobile
skin-deep (adj)
skin-dive
skin diver
skin diving
skinhead
skinny-dip
skinny-dipper
skintight
skipjack tuna
skirt steak
Skivvies ™
skiwear
skybox
skycap
skydive
skydiver
skydiving
Skye terrier
sky-high (adv, adj)
skylark
skylight
skyline
sky marshal

148

skyrocket
skyscraper
skywalk
skyway
skywrite
skywriter
skywriting
slam dunk
slaphappy
slap shot
slapstick (n, adj)
slave driver
sleazebag
sleazeball
sled dog
sledgehammer (adj, n, v)
sleep apnea
sleep-in (adj)
sleep in (v)
sleepover (n)
sleepwalk (v)
sleepwalked
sleepwalker
sleepwalking
sleight of hand
sliding scale
slimeball
slingshot
slipcover
slipknot
slip-on (n)
slipped disk
slipshod
sloe-eyed
sloe gin (fizz)
slot machine
slowdown (n)
slow down (v)
slow-footed (adj)
slow-motion (adj)

slow motion (n)
slow-pitch (n)
slowpoke
slow-witted
smack-dab
smackdown (n)
smack down (v)
smacktalk
small-cell lung cancer
small-claims court
small-fry (adj)
small-minded
small-mouth bass
smallpox
small-scale (adj)
small screen
small talk
small-time (adj)
small-timer
smart aleck (or alec)
smart-mouthed
smartphone
smarty-pants (n, adj)
smashmouth
smidgen (smidgeon, smidgin)
smithereens
smoke-filled room
smokehouse
smoke screen
smokestack
smooth fox terrier
smooth hound
s'more
smorgasbord
snack bar
snafu
snaggletooth
snaggletoothed
snail mail
snail-paced (adj)

snail's pace
snakelike
snakebite
snake charmer
snake pit
snakeskin
snapback (n)
snap back (v)
snapdragon
snap-on (adj)
snap on (v)
snapshot
snare drum
snowball
snowbank
snowbird
snow-blind (adj)
snow-blinded (adj)
snow blindness (n)
snowblower
snowboard (n, v)
snowboardcross
snowboarder
snowboarding
snowbound
snowcap
snow cone (sno-cone)
snowdrift
snowfall
snowflake
snowmobiler
snowmobiling
snowmobilist
snowplow (n, v)
snowshoe
snowstorm
snowsuit
snow-white (adj)
so-and-so
soapbox

soap opera
soapstone
soapsuds
so-called
social-minded
socioeconomic
sociopathic
sociopolitical
sockeye salmon
sofa bed
soffit
softball
softballer
soft-boiled (adj)
softcover
soft drink
softhearted
soft palate
soft-serve (n)
softshell (n)
soft-shell (adj)
soft-shelled (adj)
soft-spoken
soft spot
software
sold-out (adj)
solstice
somatosensory
someplace
somersault (summersault)
sometime (adj)
sometimes (adv)
someway (adv)
somewhat (pron, adv)
somewhere (n, adv)
somewheres (adv)
sommelier
so much as
songwriter
sonic barrier

sonic boom
son-in-law
so-so
Sotheby's ™
soul food
soulful
soul mate
soul-searching
soundalike
sound-and-light show
sound barrier
sound-bite (adj)
sound bite (n)
soundboard
soundproof
soundstage
sound wave
soup du jour
souped-up (adj)
soup kitchen
soupspoon
sourcebook
source code
sourdough
sour grapes
sourpuss
soursop
south (referring to direction)
South (referring to regions; i.e., South Florida)
southbound
southeast (referring to direction)
Southeast (referring to region; i.e., Southeast Dallas)
southeaster (storm)
Southeasterner (native of the Southeast)
southeastmost
southeastward
southerly
southern
Southerner (native of the South)
Southern Hemisphere

southernmost
southpaw
South Pole
south-southeast
south-southwest
southwest (referring to direction)
Southwest (referring to region; i.e., Southwest Dallas)
southwester
Southwesterner (native of the Southwest)
southwesternmost
southwestward
souvenir
soybean
space-age
space cadet
spaced-out (adj)
spaceflight
space heater
space out (v)
spaceship
space shuttle
space station
space suit
space walk
spanakopita
Spanglish
spaniel
Spanish onion
Spanish rice
speakeasy
speakerphone
spearfish (n, v)
speargun
spearhead
spear-thrower
Special Forces
special master
special-needs (adj)
speechless
speechwriter

speedboat
speed bump
speed dating
speed dial
speed limit
speed of light
speed-read
speed-reading
speed skater
speed skating
speed trap
speedway
spellbind
spellbinder
spellbinding
spellbound
spell-check
spell-checker
spic-and-span (or spick-and-span)
spicket (variation of spigot)
spider vein
spiderweb
spiel
spigot (also spicket)
spina bifida
spinal tap
spin doctor
spine-chilling
spin-off (n)
spin off (v)
spiral-bound
spitball
spiteful
spitfire
spitting image
splashboard
splashdown (n)
splash down (v)
splash guard
splenomegaly

split decision
split end
split-level (n, adj)
split personality
split screen
split-second (adj)
split second
spoilsport
spokesman
spokesmodel
spokespeople
spokesperson
spokeswoman
spoliation
sponge cake
sponge cloth
spoon-feed (v)
spoonful
sport fish (n)
sportfisherman
sportfishing
sportful
sports bar
sports car
sportscast
sportscaster
sportsman
sportsmanlike
sportsmanship
sports medicine
sportswear
sportswoman
sportswriter
sportswriting
sport-utility vehicle (SUV)
spot-check (v)
spotlight
spot-on (adj)
spread-eagle (v, adj)
spread eagle (n)

spreadsheet
springboard
spring chicken
spring-cleaning (n)
springer spaniel
springform pan
spring-load (v)
springtime
springwater
spumoni
spur-of-the-moment (adj)
spyglass
spymaster
spyware
squad car
squad room
squalor
squamous cell carcinoma
square off (v)
squawk box
squeaky-clean (adj)
squirrelfish
stablemate
Staffordshire bull terrier
stagecoach
stagehand
stage-manage (v)
stage management
stainless steel
staircase
stair-climber (n)
stairway
stairwell
stakeholder
stakeout (n)
stake out (v)
stalactite
stalagmite
stalemate (n)
stand-alone (adj)

standardbred
Standard English
standard-issue (adj)
standard schnauzer
standby (n, adj, adv)
stand by (v)
stand-down (n)
stand down (v)
stand-in (n)
stand in (v)
standing O
standoff (n, adj)
stand off (v)
standoffish
standout (n)
stand out (v)
standpoint
standstill (n)
stand-up (adj, n)
stand up (v)
Stanford-Binet test
staphylococcal
staphylococcus
Staples ™
star anise
starboard (n, adj, v)
Starbucks ™
starburst
starfish
star fruit
stargazer
stargazing
Star of David
starry-eyed (adj)
Stars and Stripes
star-spangled (adj)
star-studded (adj)
start-up (n)
statehouse
stateroom

state's attorney
state's evidence
States General
Stateside (adj, adv, referring to US)
statewide
static electricity
static line
stationary (nonmoving)
stationery (letter paper)
station house
stationmaster
status quo
statute book
statute of limitations
stay-at-home (adj)
staycation
steadfast
steak house
steamboat
steamer trunk
steamfitter
steamroller
steamship
steelmaker
steelmaking
steelworker
steelyard
steeplechase
steering wheel
stem cell
stenosis
step aerobics
stepbrother
step-by-step (adj, adv)
stepchild
stepdaughter
step-down (n)
step down (v)
stepfamily
stepfather

stepgrandmother
step-in (n)
step in (v)
stepkids
stepladder
stepmom
stepmother
stepparent
stepping-stone (n) (steppingstone)
stepsister
step stool
step-up (n, adj)
step up (v)
stepwise
stick-in-the-mud (n)
stickman
stickpin
stick shift
stick-to-itiveness
sticky note
stillbirth
stillborn
still life
still lifes
Stilton (cheese)
stingray
stinkbug
stir-crazy (adj)
stir-fry (n, v)
stirrup
stock boy
stockbroker
stock car
stockholder
Stockholm syndrome
stockkeeper
stock market
stock option
stockpile
stockpot

stockroom
stockyard
stomachache
stone-cold (adv)
stone crab
stonefish
stone-ground (adj)
stone's throw
stoneware
stonewashed
stonework
stop-and-go (adj)
stopgap
stoplight
stopwatch
store-bought (adj)
storefront (n, adj)
storekeeper
storeroom
storewide
storyboard
storybook (n, adj)
story line
storyteller
stowaway (n)
stow away (v)
strabismus
straight-ahead (adj)
straight and narrow (n)
straightaway (adv, adj, n)
straightedge (n)
straight face (n)
straight-faced (adj)
straight flush
straightforward
straight-line (adj)
straight shooter
straitjacket (straightjacket)
straitlaced (straightlaced)
stranglehold

straw man
streamline (n, v)
streetcar
street fighter
street hockey
streetlight
street-smart (adj)
street smarts (n)
streetwise
strep throat
stressed-out (adj)
stretch marks
strikeout (n)
stroke out (v)
strokeover
strike zone
striking distance
stringpiece
stripped-down (adj)
strip search
strong-arm (adj, v)
stronghold
strong-minded (adj)
strongpoint (n)
strong suit (n)
stuccowork
stun gun
stuntman
stuntwoman
stylebook
Styrofoam ™
subarachnoid
subclavian
subconscious
subcontract
subcutaneous
subdivision
subdural
sublease
sublet

subpoena duces tecum
subprime
sub-Saharan
subsection
subterranean
successful
succotash
sucker punch
suck-up (adj)
sugarcane
sugarcoat
sugar daddy
sugarload
sugarplum
sui generis
sui juris
summa cum laude
summerhouse
sumerlong
summertime
summing-up (n)
sump pump
sum-up (n)
sum up (v)
sunbaked
sunbathe
sunbather
sunbeam
sunblock
sunbonnet
sunburn
sunburst
Sunday-go-to-meeting
Sunday school
sundeck
sundew
sundial
sundown
sundress
sunflower

sunglasses
sun goddess
sunlight
sunlit
sunny-side up
sunrise
sunscreen
sunseeker
sunshade
sunshine
sunstroke
sunup (n)
supercharger
supercool
super-duper
superfluous
superglue
superheavyweight
superhero
superhigh frequency
superhighway
superhuman
superimpose
supermarket
superminicomputer
superpower
superscript
supersede
supersize (v)
supersonic
superstar
superstore
superwoman
suprarenal gland
supraventricular
surefire
sure-footed (adj)
sure-footedness
sure-handed
sure-handedness

surface-to-air (adj)
surfactant
surfboard
surfboat
surgeon's knot
surmount
surname
surpass
surrebuttal
surrebutter
Sussex spaniel
sustained-release
SUV (sport-utility vehicle)
swamp buggy
swan dive
swan song
swashbuckler
swearword
sweatbox
sweaterdress
sweater-vest
sweatpants
sweatshirt
sweatshop
sweat suit
Swedish massage
sweepstakes
sweet-and-sour (adj)
sweet-talk (v)
sweet talk (n)
swelled head
swelled-headed
swelled-headedness
swimmer's ear
swimsuit
swimwear
swine flu
swing shift
Swiss chard
Swiss cheese

switchblade
switchboard
switcheroo
switch-hit
switch-hitter
switch knife
swizzle stick
swordfish
symptomatology
syncope

—T—

Tabasco ™
tabbouleh (tabouleh)
tablecloth
tableful
tablespoon
tablespoonful
table tennis
tabletop
tableware
tachometer
tachyarrhythmia
tachycardia
taciturn
tackboard
tackiness
tae kwon do
tagalong (n)
tag along (v)
tagline
tag team
tai chi
tailbone
tailcoat
tailgate (n, v)
tailgater
tailgating
taillight
tailor-made

tailpipe
tailspin
takeaway (n, adj)
take-charge (adj)
takedown (n, adj)
take down (v)
take-home pay
take-no-prisoners (adj)
takeoff (n)
take off (v)
takeout (n)
take-out (adj)
take out (v)
takeover (n)
take over (v)
talcum powder
taleggio (cheese)
talking head
talking-to (n)
talk radio
talk show
tallyho
tangential
Tango   (communications code for T)
tankini
tank top
tantamount
tape-record (v)
tape recorder
tape recording
taperstick
tapeworm
tap-in (golf)
tap out (v)
tapped out
taproom
tap water
tar paper
tartaric acid
tartar sauce

TASER ™
Tasmanian devil
taste bud
tasteful
tasteless
tattletale
tawdry
taximeter
taxicab
taxpayer
taxpaying
tax shelter
Tay-Sachs disease
T-ball
T-bone
T cell
tchotchke (chotchke)
tea bag
tea ball
teacher's pet
teacup
teahouse
teakettle
teakwood
teammate
teamster
teamwork
teardrop
tearful
tear gas (n, v)
tearjerker
tear-jerking
tea set
teaspoon
teatime
tea towel
tea tray
tea tree
Technicolor ™
technobabble

techno-pop
tectonic
tee-hee
teenage
teensy-weensy
teenybop
teenybopper
teeny-weeny
tee off
teepee
teeterboard
teethridge
teetotaler
Teflon ™
telecast
telecaster
telecom
telecommunication
telecommute
telecommuter
teleconferencing
Telecopier ™
telefax
telegram
telegraph
telekinesis
telemarketer
telemarketing
telenovela
teleport
teleprocessing
teleprompter
telescope
teletypewriter
televangelist
television
tell-all
telltale
temerity
temperament

temporal bone
temporal lobe
temporomandibular
tenaculum
tenderhearted
tender-minded
tendinitis
tendon of Achilles
tenement house
tenpenny nail
TENS (transcutaneous electrical nerve stimulation)
teppanyaki
terabyte
teratocarcinoma
teriyaki
terrazzo
terrier
tertiary care
testator
testatrix
test-drive (n, v)
test-driven
test-driving
test-drove
test-market (v)
test-tube (adj)
test tube (n)
tetherball
Texas Hold'em
Tex-Mex
textbook
T formation (football)
T4 cell
thankful
thankless
thank-you (n)
thataway
ThD (Doctor or Theology)
third world country
third-party (adj)

third party (n)
theatergoer
theirselves
thereabouts
thereafter
thereby
therefor
therefore
thereinafter
thereof
thereon
thereto
theretofore
thereunder
thereunto
thereupon
therewith
therewithal
thermoelectricity
thermonuclear
thermostat
thickheaded
thick-skinned
thighbone
thigh-slapper
thingamabob
thingamajig
thing-in-itself
things-in-themselves
think tank
thin-skinned
third-class (adj, adv)
third class (n)
third degree (n)
third-degree (adj)
third dimension
third-dimensional
thirdhand
third-party (adj)
third party (n)

third person
third-rate (adj)
Third World
thirtysomething
thoroughbred
thoroughfare
Thousand Island dressing
3-D
three-dimensional
threefold
three-legged (adj)
three of a kind
three-peat
threepence
three-point turn
three-ring circus
threesome
three-wheeler
throughout
throwaway (n, adj)
throw away (v)
throwback (n)
throw back (v)
thumbnail
thumbprint
thumbs-down (n)
thumbs-up (n)
thumbtack
thundercloud
thundershower
thunderstorm
thyroid-stimulating hormone
tib-fib fracture (not in dictionaries, used often)
tibiofibula
tick-borne (adj)
tick fever
ticktock
tic-tac-toe
tidal wave
tidbit

tidewater
tieback (n)
tie back (v)
tiebreaker
tie-down (n)
tie-dye
tie-dyed
tie-dyeing
tie-in (n)
tie in (v)
tie-line (n)
tight end
tightfisted
tight-knit
tight-lipped
tight-mouthed
tightrope
tightwad
tightwire
tighty-whities (tighty-whiteys)
tiki bar
tilt-rotor
time and a half (n)
time card
time clock
time-consuming
time-release
timed-release
time frame (timeframe)
timekeeper
timekeeping
time-lapse (adj)
time lag
timeless
time line (timeline)
time-out (n)
timepiece
time-saving (adj)
time-saver (n)
time-share (n)

time-sharing (n)
time sheet (n)
time stamp (n)
time-stamp (v)
timetable (n)
time-table (v)
time-tested (adj)
time zone
Tinseltown
tiptoe
tip-top (n, adj, adv)
tiramisu
tireless
tiresome
tit for tat (adv)
tit-for-tat (adj)
titleholder
TiVo ™
T-Mobile ™
T-note
toadstool
toboggan
tobogganer
tobogganing
toenail
toe the line
toe-to-toe (adj, adv)
toilet paper
tollbooth
toll call
toll-free
tollgate
tollhouse
Toll House ™
tomahawk
tombstone
Tom Collins (cocktail)
tomfoolery
tomography
tom-tom (drum)

tone-deaf
tongue-in-cheek (adj)
tongue in cheek
tongue-lash (v)
tongue-lashing (n)
tongue-tie (v)
tongue-tied
tongue twister
toolbar
toolbox
toolroom
toolshed
toothache
tooth and nail
toothbrush
toothpaste
toothsome
toothsomeness
topcoat
top dollar
top-end (adj)
Top 40
top-heavy (adj)
top-notch (adj)
topnotcher
top-of-the-line (adj)
top-shelf (adj)
topside (n, adj, adv)
Top-Sider ™
topsoil
topsy-turviness
topsy-turvy (n, adv, adj)
torchbearer
torticollis
tortoiseshell
toss-up (n)
totalitarian
touchback (n)
touchdown (n)
touch down (v)

touch screen
touch-tone
touch-up (n)
touch up (v)
touchy-feely
Tourette's syndrome
tow-away zone
towboat
to wit
town car
town crier
town hall
townhome
town house
townscape
townsman
townspeople
townswoman
toxic shock syndrome
toy Manchester terrier
Toyota 4Runner ™
Toyota RAV4 ™
toy poodle
track-and-field (adj)
trackball
track lighting
track record
tracksuit
tractor-trailer
trade-in (n)
trade in (v)
trademark
trade-off (n)
trafficked
trafficking
trailblazer
trail mix
trajectory
transaxle
trans-fatty acid

transient ischemic attack
translucent
transpacific
traveler's check
treadmill
treble damages (law)
tree frog
tree house
treetop
trelliswork
trench coat
trendsetter
trendsetting
triceps
trickle-down theory
tricuspid
tried-and-true (adj)
trifecta
trifocal
trigeminal nerve
trigger-happy (adj)
triggerman
trigger point (n)
triple-decker (adj)
triple-header (n)
triple play
triple sec
trip wire
tristate
triweekly
Trojan horse
trolleybus
troublemaker
troubleshoot
troubleshooter
troubleshooting
troublesome
truckline
truckload
truck stop

true-false test
truehearted
true-life (adj)
truelove (n)
trumped-up (adj)
truncate
trundle bed
trust fund
trustworthy
truthful
truth-value (n)
tsk-tsk
tubal ligation
tune-up (n)
tuning fork
tunnel vision
tunnel-visioned
turbojet
turbojet engine
turboprop
turboprop engine
turboshaft
turnaround (n)
turn around (v)
turncoat
turndown (adj, n)
turn down (v)
Turner's syndrome
turn-in (n)
turn in (v)
turnkey (adj, n)
turnoff (n)
turn off (v)
turnout (n)
turn out (v)
turnover (adj, n)
turn over (v)
turnstile
turntable
turnup (adj, n)

turn up (v)
turtledove
turtlehead
turtleneck
tuttelage
tutti-frutti
Tweedledum and Tweedledee
12-step
24/7
twentysomething
twin-size (adj)
twist tie
two-bit
two-by-four
two-dimensional
two-door (adj)
two-edged sword
two-faced
twofer
two-fisted
twofold
two-handed
twopence
two-piece (adj, n)
two-ply
two-point turn
two-sided
twosome
two-step (n, v)
two-time
two-tone
two-way (adj)
two-wheeler
TYLENOL ™
type A
type B
typecast
typeface
type 1 diabetes
typeset

typesetter
typesetting
type 2 diabetes
typewrite
typewriter
typewriting
typhoid fever
typographic
typographical

—U—

uh-huh
uh-oh
uh-uh
ukulele (ukelele)
ultrabook
ultrahazardous
ultrahigh frequency
ultralight
ultra-pasteurized
ultrasonographer
ultrasonography
ultrasound
ultraviolet
umbilical cord
umpteen
umpteenth
unabashed
unabridged
unadulterated
unaffected
un-American
unbeknownst
uncalled-for (adj)
uncleanliness
unconscionable
unconscious
uncouth

unctuous
underachiever
underactive
underage (n, adj)
underarm
under armor (protective sports gear)
Under Armour ™ (brand of sports clothing)
underbelly
underbid
undercarriage
underclass
undercoat
undercover (n, adj)
undercurrent
underdeveloped
underestimate
undergraduate
underhanded
underpass
underprivileged
underscore
undersigned
understaffed
underwhelm
underwriter
unencumbered
unequivocally
unfaithful
unfathomable
unfettered
unfurl
unheard-of (adj)
Uniform (communications code for U)
UnitedHealthcare ™
Universal Product Code
unknowingly
unpretentious
unrealistic
unrelenting
unselfish

unsportsmanlike
untruthful
unveiled
unwittingly
unyielding
up-and-coming
up-and-comer
up-and-down (adj)
up and down (adv)
up-and-up (n)
upbringing
upchuck
upcoming
up-front (adj)
up front
upgrade
upheaval
upholstery
upload
uppercase
upper class (n)
upper-class (adj)
upperclassman
uppercut (boxing)
upper hand
uppermost
upright
uprise
uprising
uproar
ups and downs
upscale
upside down (adv)
upside-down (adj)
upstage (adv, adj, v, n)
upstanding
upstream
upswing
uptake
up-to-date (adj)

up-to-the-minute (adj)
urogenital
urogynecology
urolithiasis
Ursa Major
Ursa Minor
user-friendliness
user-friendly
utmost
U-turn

—V—

vacuum
vacuum-packed
vagabond
vagus nerve
valedictorian
Valencia orange
valgus
Valley girl
Valsalva maneuver
value-added (adj)
value-free (adj)
vancomycin
vantage point
variegated
vas deferens
Vaseline ™
vasoconstrictive
vasoconstrictor
vasodilator
vasomotor
vasopressin
vasopressor
vasovagal
vehement
Velcro ™
vena cava
venipuncture
ventriloquist

venture capital
venture capitalism
venture capitalist
vernacular
Victor   (communications code for V)
Vidalia   (certification mark, onion)
video camera
videocassette
video game
videophone
videotape
viewfinder
viewpoint
vineyard
violoncello
vis-à-vis
Vise-Grip ™
visual acuity
visual cortex
visual field
vitreous humor
voice box
voiceful
voiceless
voice mail (voicemail)
voice-over
VoIP (Voice over Internet Protocol)
voir dire
volleyball
volt-ampere
voltmeter
vo-tech

—W—

wage earner
wainscot
wainscoted
wainscoting
waistband
waistline

wait-list (v)
waitperson
waitress
waitstaff
wakeboard
wake-up (adj)
wake up (v)
Waldorf salad
Walgreens ™ (store name)
Walgreen Co. ™ (corporate name)
walkie-talkie
walk-in (adj, n)
walk-through (n, also walk-thru)
walk-up (adj, n)
walkway
wallflower
wallpaper
wall-to-wall (adj)
Walmart ™ (store name)
Wal-Mart ™ (corporate name)
want ad
wanton (lacking discipline)
warhead
warhorse
warlike
warlock
warlord
warm-blooded
warmed-over
warm-up (adj, n)
warm up (v)
warpath
warplane
warp speed (n)
warp-speed (adj)
warship
warthog
wartime
warts-and-all (adj)
wash-and-wear (adj)

washbasin
washboard
washcloth
washed-out (adj)
washed-up (adj)
washout (n)
wash out (v)
washrag
washroom
washtub
wastebasket
wastepaper
waste pipe
wastewater
watchband
watchdog
watchful
watchmaker
watchmaking
watchtower
waterboarding
waterborne
watercolor
watercooler
watercress
waterfall
waterfront
water gun
water heater
water lily
waterline
waterlogged
water main
watermark
watermelon
water moccasin
water park
water pipe
waterproof
water-repellent

water-resistant
watershed
water ski (n)
water-ski (v)
water-skier (n)
waterskiing
waterslide
water spaniel
waterspout
watertight
water tower
waterway
waterworks
watt-hour
wave crest
wavelength
ways and means
wayside
weakhearted
weak-kneed
weak-minded
wearisome
weather-beaten
weatherboard
weather-bound
weathercast
weathercaster
weatherglass
weatherman
weatherperson
weatherproof
weather vane
webcam
webcast
webfoot
webinar
webisode
Web log (known as a blog)
webmaster
Web site (website)

webwork
Wedgwood ™
wedlock
Weed Eater ™
Weedwacker ™
weekday
weekend
weekend warrior
weeklong
weeknight
weeping willow
weigh-in (n)
weigh in (v)
weight lifter
weight lifting
weight training
Weimaraner (dog)
weisenheimer
well-adjusted
well-advised
well-appointed
well-balanced
well-being
well-done
well-founded
well-heeled
well-known
well-meaning
well-meant
well-oiled
well-rounded
well-spoken
well-thought-of
well-to-do
well-wisher
Welsh corgi
Welsh rabbit (also rarebit)
Welsh springer spaniel
Welsh terrier
welterweight

werewolf
Wernicke's area
west (referring to direction)
West (referring to regions; i.e., West New York)
westbound
Westerner (one who lives in the West)
Western Hemisphere
westernmost
Western Union ™
Westlaw ™
West Nile virus
west-northwest
west-southwest
westward
wet bar
wetland
wet-nurse (v)
wet nurse (n)
wet suit
wharfmaster
whatchamacallit
what-if (n, adj)
whatnot
whatsoever
wheat germ
wheatgrass
wheelbarrow
wheelbase
wheelchair
whereabouts
whereas
whereby
wherefore
wherefrom
wherein
whereof
whereon
whereto
whereupon
wherewithal

whiplash
whippersnapper
whippet
whip-poor-will (bird)
whirlpool
Whiskey (communications code for W)
whistle-blower
whistle-blowing
whistle-stop (n, v)
whiteboard
whitecap (wave crest with white foam)
white-coat hypertension
white-collar (adj)
whitefish
white-hot (adj)
white-knuckle (adj)
white-knuckled (adj)
whiteout (extreme weather usu. snow)
white pages
White Russian (cocktail)
whitewash
whitewashing
white water (n)
white-water (adj)
white zinfandel
whiz kid
wholehearted
wholeheartedly
whole-life (adj)
wholesome
whoop-de-do (whoop-de-doo)
whoopee cushion
whooping cough
whooping crane
wide-angle (adj)
wide area network
wide-body (n, aircraft)
wide-eyed
widemouthed
wide-open (adj)

wide-ranging (adj)
wide receiver
wide-screen (adj)
widespread
widget
Wiener schnitzel
Wi-Fi
wildcard
wildebeest
willful
willful and wanton
Williams-Sonoma ™
willpower
willy-nilly (willynilly)
windblown
wind-borne
Windbreaker ™
windburn
windchill
wind-chill factor
wind chime
windfall
windjammer
windjamming
windmill
windowdressing
windowpane
windowshop
windowshopper
windowsill
windpipe
windproof
windshield
windstorm
Windsurfer ™
windsurfer (person using Windsurfer)
windsurfing
windup (adj, n)
wind up (v)
windward

wine cellar
wine cooler
wineglass
winegrower
winemaker
winepress
wineshop
wine taster
wingback
wingding
wing nut
wingspan
wintertime
win-win
wire fox terrier
wirehaired terrier
wiretap
wisecrack
wise guy
wishbone
wishy-washy
witchcraft
witches' brew
witch hazel
witch hunt
witch-hunter
witch-hunting
Wite-Out ™ (Bic's brand of correction fluid)
withindoors (indoors)
withoutdoors (outdoors)
witness stand
wittiness
woeful
womanlike
women's rights
women's room
women's wear
wonton
woodblock
wood carving

woodchuck
woodpecker
woodstove
woodwork
woodworking
woo-hoo
woolly mammoth
Worcestershire sauce
word-association test
wordbook
word-for-word (adj)
word for word (adv)
wordmonger
word-mongering
word-of-mouth (adj)
wordsmith
workbook
workday
workers' compensation
workfolk
workforce
workhorse
working capital
working-class (adj)
working class (n)
working dog
workload
workmanlike
workmanship
workpeople
workpiece
workplace
workroom
workshop
workspace
workstation
work-study program
worktable
workup (n)
work up (v)

workweek
world-class (adj)
worldly-minded
World Wide Web
worrisome
worst-case (adj)
would-be (adj)
wraparound (adj, n)
wristband
wristlet
wristwatch
write-off (n)
write off (v)
writer's block
writer's cramp
write-up (n)
write up (v)
writ of certiorari (law)
writ of habeas corpus (law)
writ of mandamus
writ of summons
wrongdoer
wrongdoing

—X—

Xanadu
x-axis
X chromosome
x-coordinate
xenograft
xenolith
Xerox ™
X factor
XFINITY ™
x-height
xiphoid
x-irradiation
x-radiation
X-rated
x-ray (v)

X-ray (n)
Xray (communication code for letter X)
X-ray astronomy
X-ray diffraction
X-ray star
X-ray therapy
X-ray tube
x-section

—Y—

yachtsman
yada yada (yadda yadda)
Yahoo! ™
Yankee (communications code for Y)
yardbird
yardman
yardmaster
yard sale
yardstick
yaw mark (industry term)
y-axis
yay (used as a cheer)
Y chromosome
y-coordinate
yea (used in taking votes)
yea big
yea high
yearbook
year-end (n, adj)
yearlong
year-round (adj)
yea-sayer
yellowfin tuna
yenta
yeshivah
yes-man (n)
yesteryear
Yinglish
y-intercept
yolk sac

Yom Kippur
yoo-hoo
Yorkie
Yorkshire pudding
Yorkshire terrier
yottabyte
you-all
youngblood
young Turk
YouTube ™
yo-yo
yule
Yule log
yuletide

—Z—

Zamboni ™
z-axis
z-coordinate
z distribution
Zen
zenith
zephyr
zigzag
zigzagging
zinfandel
ZIP code (zip code)
zip line
ziplock
Ziploc ™
zonked-out (adj)
zookeeper
zoom lens
zooplankton
zoot suit
zucchini
Zulu (communications code for Z)
zygomatic process